HIGHER

Practice Book

MASTERING → MATHEMAT

FOR

WJEC GCSE

Practice • Reinforcement • Progress

Assessment Consultant and Editor: **Keith Pledger**

Keith Pledger, Gareth Cole, Joe Petran and Linda Mason

Series Editor: Roger Porkess

HODDER
EDUCATION
AN HACHETTE UK COMPANY

Photo credits

p.145 © Ingram Publishing – Thinkstock/Getty Images; p.146 © Lana Langlois – 123RF.

Although every effort has been made to ensure that website addresses are correct at time of going to press, Hodder Education cannot be held responsible for the content of any website mentioned. It is sometimes possible to find a relocated web page by typing in the address of the home page for a website in the URL window of your browser.

Orders: please contact Bookpoint Ltd, 130 Milton Park, Abingdon, Oxon OX14 4SB. Telephone: (44) 01235 827720. Fax: (44) 01235 400454. Lines are open 9.00–17.00, Monday to Saturday, with a 24-hour message answering service. Visit our website at www.hoddereducation.co.uk.

© Keith Pledger, Gareth Cole, Joe Petran, Linda Mason 2016

First published in 2016 by

Hodder Education

An Hachette UK Company,

50 Victoria Embankment

London EC4Y 0DZ

Impression number	5	4	3	2	1
Year	2020	2019	2018	2017	2016

Cover photo © ShpilbergStudios

Illustrations by Integra

Typeset in India by Integra Software Services Pvt. Ltd., Pondicherry

Printed in Great Britain by CPI Group (UK) Ltd, Croydon CR0 4YY

A catalogue record for this title is available from the British Library.

ISBN 978 1471 874628

Contents

Units with this symbol are required for the Mathematics GCSE only.

NUMBER

Strand 2 Using our number system

Strand 3 Accuracy

Strand 5 Percentages

Strand 6 Ratio and proportion

Strand 7 Number properties

ALGEBRA

Strand 1 Starting algebra

Strand 2 Sequences

Strand 3 Functions and graphs

Strand 4 Algebraic methods

Strand 5 Working with quadratics

Strand 6 Properties of non-linear graphs

Use of Algebra in proportion included in Number Strand 6 Units 4–6

GEOMETRY AND MEASURES

Strand 1 Units and scales

Strand 2 Properties of shapes

Strand 3 Measuring shapes

Strand 4 Construction

Strand 5 Transformations

Strand 6 3D shapes

STATISTICS AND PROBABILITY

Strand 1 Statistical measures

Strand 2 Statistical diagrams

Strand 3 Collecting data

Strand 4 Probability

How to get the most from this book

Introduction

This book is part of the Mastering Mathematics for WJEC GCSE series and supports the textbook by providing lots of extra practice questions for the Higher tier in Mathematics and Mathematics–Numeracy.

This Practice Book is structured to match the Higher Student's Book and is likewise organised by key areas of the specification: Number, Algebra, Geometry & Measures and Statistics & Probability. Every chapter in this book accompanies its corresponding chapter from the textbook, with matching titles for ease of use.

Please note: the 'Moving On' units in the Student's Book cover prior knowledge only, so do not have accompanying chapters in this Practice Book. For this reason, although the running order of the Practice Book follows the Student's Book, you may notice that some Strand/Unit numbers appear to be missing, or do not start at '1'.

Progression through each chapter

Chapters include a range of questions that increase in difficulty as you progress through the exercise. There are three levels of difficulty across the Student's Books and Practice Books in this series. These are denoted by shaded spots on the right hand side of each page. Levels broadly reflect GCSE Maths grades as follows:

Low difficulty   GCSE Maths grades C–B   ● ○ ○

Medium difficulty   GCSE Maths grades B–A   ● ● ○

High difficulty   GCSE Maths grades A–A*   ● ● ●

You might wish to start at the beginning of each chapter and work through so you can see how you are progressing.

Question types

There is also a range of question types included in each chapter, which are denoted by codes to the left hand side of the question or sub-question where they appear. These are examples of the types of question that you will need to practice in readiness for the GCSE Maths Higher exam.

PS Practising skills

These questions are all about building and mastering the essential techniques that you need to succeed.

DF Developing fluency

These give you practice of using your skills for a variety of purposes and contexts, building your confidence to tackle any type of question.

PB Problem solving

These give practice of using your problem solving skills in order to tackle more demanding problems in the real world, in other subjects and within Maths itself.

Next to any question, including the above question types, you may also see the below code. This means that it is an exam-style question

ES Exam style

This question reflects the language, style and wording of a question that you might see in your GCSE Maths Higher exam.

Answers

There are answers to every question within the book on our website.

Please visit: www.hoddereducation.co.uk/MasteringmathsforWJECGCSE

Number Strand 2 Using our number system Unit 7 Calculating with standard form

PS — PRACTISING SKILLS   DF — DEVELOPING FLUENCY   PB — PROBLEM SOLVING   ES — EXAM-STYLE

PS **1** Copy and complete each of the following. Replace each letter with the missing number.

a $5.85 \times 10^5 + 2.35 = a \times 10^5$

b $1.97 \times 10^{-3} + 2.8 \times 10^{-3} = b \times 10^{-3}$

c $7.09 \times 10^7 - 6.3 \times 10^7 = c \times 10^8$

d $9.4 \times 10^{-5} + 9.4 \times 10^{-5} = d \times 10^{-4}$

PS **2** Work out the following, giving your answers in standard form.

a $100 \times 1.8 \times 10^6$
b $1000 \times 9.3 \times 10^7$

c $10000 \times 2.7 \times 10^{-2}$
d $5.3 \times 10^7 \div 1000$

e $1.03 \times 10^3 \div 10000$
f $1.2 \times 10^{-4} \div 100$

DF **3** Given that $x = 3.5 \times 10^5$, $y = 1.8 \times 10^2$ and $z = 2 \times 10^{-3}$, work out the value of the following. Give your answers in standard form.

a xy
b $\dfrac{x}{z}$

c x^2
d z^3

e xyz
f x^{-3}

DF **4** Use the information in the table to answer the following. Give your answers in standard form.

1 kilowatt = 10^3 watts	
1 megawatt = 10^6 watts	
1 gigawatt = 10^9 watts	
1 terawatt = 10^{12} watts	

a Change 230 gigawatts to watts.

b Change 0.25 gigawatts to kilowatts.

c Change 125 kilowatts to megawatts.

d Change 18500 megawatts to terawatts.

DF

5 The mass of a blue whale is 1.9×10^5 kg.

The mass of a house mouse is 1.9×10^{-2} kg.

How many times greater than the mass of the house mouse is the mass of the blue whale?

DF

6 Scientists estimate:

- there are about 100 billion galaxies in the observable universe and
- each galaxy contains an average of 300 billion stars.

Work out an estimate for the total number of stars in the observable universe.

Give your answer in standard form.

(1 billion = 10^9)

DF

ES

7 The table gives information about the number of litres of water used by a factory for seven days.

Monday	Tuesday	Wednesday	Thursday	Friday	Saturday	Sunday
9.32×10^5	9.85×10^5	1.02×10^6	9.93×10^5	1.18×10^6	1.05×10^6	9.66×10^5

Work out the mean amount of water the factory uses each day.

Give your answer in litres, in standard form.

DF

8 $x = 4.5 \times 10^4$

For each of the following, give your answer in standard form correct to four decimal places.

a Work out

i x^3 **ii** $\sqrt[3]{x}$ **iii** $\frac{1}{x}$.

b What number is half way between x and $\sqrt{x}$?

PB

ES

9 The speed of light is approximately 3×10^8 m/s and the distance of the Earth from the Sun is approximately 1.5×10^{11} m.

Approximately how many seconds does it take for light to travel from the Sun to the Earth?

PB

ES

10 The diagram shows a circle drawn inside a square.

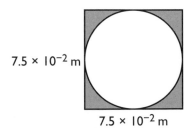

7.5×10^{-2} m

7.5×10^{-2} m

Work out the area, in m², of the shaded part.

Give your answer in standard form correct to 3 significant figures.

Number Strand 2 Using our number system
Unit 8 Recurring decimals

PS ▸ PRACTISING SKILLS   **DF** ▸ DEVELOPING FLUENCY   **PB** ▸ PROBLEM SOLVING   **ES** ▸ EXAM-STYLE

PS **1** Which of these fractions can be written as a recurring decimal?

   a $\dfrac{1}{3}$

   b $\dfrac{3}{6}$

   c $\dfrac{1}{15}$

   d $\dfrac{7}{20}$

   e $\dfrac{2}{13}$

PS **2** Convert these recurring decimals into fractions.

   a $0.\dot{7}$

   b $0.\dot{5}$

   c $0.\dot{1}\dot{3}$

   d $0.4\dot{5}$

   e $0.\dot{1}5\dot{1}$

DF **3** Write these recurring decimals as fractions.

   a $0.\dot{4}$

   b $0.0\dot{4}$

   c $0.00\dot{4}$

   d $0.0\dot{1}0\dot{4}$

   e $5.000\dot{4}$

DF **4** **a** Write down the recurring decimals for $\frac{1}{13}, \frac{3}{13}, \frac{4}{13}, \frac{9}{13}, \frac{10}{13}, \frac{12}{13}$.

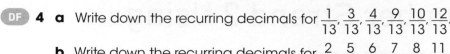

b Write down the recurring decimals for $\frac{2}{13}, \frac{5}{13}, \frac{6}{13}, \frac{7}{13}, \frac{8}{13}, \frac{11}{13}$.

c Explain what you notice between the two sets of fractions.

PE **5** Seventeenths also have a pattern of repeating digits in their recurring decimals. There are 16 digits in the pattern.
Work out the order of the digits. You must show your working.

PE **6** Given that $0.\dot{4} = \frac{4}{9}$, express the recurring decimal $0.6\dot{4}$ as a fraction.
FS

PE **7** Explain why $9.\dot{9} = 10$.
FS

PE **8** Explain why any fraction of the form $\frac{1}{p}$ where p is a prime number
FS can be written as a recurring decimal when p is not 2 or 5, and why the number of digits in the recurring pattern is always less than p.
Give an example.

DF **9** Convert each of these recurring decimals into a fraction in its simplest form.

a $0.\dot{5}$

b $0.7\dot{5}$

c $0.0\dot{2}\dot{5}$

d $0.3\dot{2}3\dot{5}$

e $5.1\dot{2}0\dot{5}$

Number Strand 3 Accuracy
Unit 6 Significance

PS — PRACTISING SKILLS   DF — DEVELOPING FLUENCY   PB — PROBLEM SOLVING   ES — EXAM-STYLE

PS **1** Write down the number of significant figures there are in each
of these numbers.

   a 2.75

   b 507

   c 0.0045

   d 1009

   e 0.0306

   f 1.0

PS **2** Write these numbers to two significant figures.

   a 2.75

   b 507

   c 0.004 53

   d 1009

   e 0.0306

   f 1.02

PS **3** Write the number 2 367 450 correct to

   a three significant figures

   b one significant figure

   c two significant figures.

PS **4** Write the number 0.399 99 correct to

   a three significant figures

   b one significant figure

   c two significant figures.

PB **5** 17845 people attended an outdoor concert in a park.

    a The local newspaper gave the attendance to three significant figures. Write the attendance to three significant figures.

    b The local Radio station gave the attendance to two significant figures. Write the attendance to two significant figures.

    c The local TV reporter gave the attendance to one significant figure. Write the attendance to one significant figure.

PB **6** The formula for working out the area of an ellipse is πab.

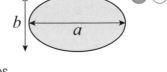

    a Using the value of π as 3.141 59, find the area of the ellipse where $a = 4.50$ and $b = 2.76$. Give the answer correct to three significant figures.

    b Find the difference in the answer to part **a** and the answer if the value of π being used was written to three significant figures. Give the answer correct to three significant figures.

PB **7** Here is part of Gerri's gas bill. It shows the units she used during March.

Work out Gerri's gas bill for March. Give your answer correct to two significant figures.

Gas 2U	
Mrs G Hall	April 4th
2 High St	
End of March reading	4593
End of February reading	3976
Units used	617
Cost per unit	15.6 pence
Monthly charge	£10.50

PB
ES **8** The Earth is 92955807miles away from the Sun. The speed of light is 186000 miles per second correct to 3 significant figures.

Find the number of seconds it takes for a ray of light to leave the Sun and reach the Earth. Give your answer correct to two significant figures.

DF
ES **9** The area of a square is 8 cm².

Find the length of one side of the square.
Give your answer correct to three siginificant figures.

8 cm²

DF
ES **10** The volume of a cube is 10 cm³.

Find the length of one side of the cube.
Give your answer correct to three significant figures.

10 cm³

PS
ES **11** Paula ran 10.55 miles in 1 hour 54 minutes.

Work out her average speed in miles per hour. Give your answer correct to two significant figures.

Number Strand 3 Accuracy
Unit 7 Limits of accuracy

PS — PRACTISING SKILLS   **DF** — DEVELOPING FLUENCY   **PB** — PROBLEM SOLVING   **ES** — EXAM-STYLE

PS **1** Write down the lower and upper bounds for each of these measurements.

   a 2300 m (to the nearest m)

   b 2300 m (to the nearest 10 m)

   c 2300 m (to the nearest 50 m)

PS **2** Each of these measurements is rounded to the number of decimal places given in brackets.
Write down the lower and upper bounds for each measurement.

   a 7.8 ml (to 1 decimal place)

   b 0.3 ml (to 1 decimal place)

   c 0.31 m (to 2 decimal places)

   d 0.058 m (to 3 decimal places)

PS **3** Each of these measurements is rounded to the given number of significant figures.
Write down the lower and upper bounds for each measurement.

   a 9 g (to 1 significant figure)

   b 90 g (to 1 significant figure)

   c 84 cm (to 2 significant figures)

   d 0.84 cm (to 2 significant figures)

PS **4** Copy and complete the inequality statement for each part.

   a The length of a ladder is x cm. To the nearest 10 cm, the length is 370 cm.
     $\boxed{} \leqslant x < \boxed{}$

   b The mass of an egg is m g. To the nearest gram, the mass is 57 g.
     $\boxed{} \leqslant m < \boxed{}$

   c The body temperature of a baby is T °C. To 1 decimal place, the temperature is 36.4 °C.
     $\boxed{} \leqslant T < \boxed{}$

   d The capacity of a saucepan is y litres. To 2 significant figures, the capacity is 2.8 litres.
     $\boxed{} \leqslant y < \boxed{}$

DF **5** $x = 56.7$ (to 1 decimal place) and $y = 84.2$ (to 1 decimal place).

  a Work out the lower bound for x.

  b Work out the lower bound for y.

  c Work out the lower bound for $x + y$.

DF **6** A square field has side length 65 m, to the nearest metre.
Work out the lower and upper bounds for

  a the perimeter of the square

  b the area of the square.

DF **7** Given that $23.5 \leqslant l < 24.5$ and $17.5 \leqslant m < 18.5$, work out the upper bound for $l - m$.

PB **8** A stadium sells premium tickets and standard tickets.

ES The cost of a premium ticket is £25.00.
The cost of a standard ticket is £12.50.
On Saturday:

  • 2500 people buy a premium ticket (to the nearest 100)

  • 7400 people buy a standard ticket (to the nearest 100).

Let T be the total amount of money paid for premium tickets and standard tickets.
Work out the lower bound and the upper bound for T.

PB **9** Alis recorded the time taken, to the nearest 10 seconds, for a cashier to serve each of four customers in a shop.

ES Here are her results.

150   220   190   110

Work out the lower bound for the mean time taken to serve these customers.

PB **10** The diagram shows a badge that is in the shape of a sector of a circle.

The radius of the sector of the circle is 8.6 cm (to 2 significant figures).
Work out

  a the upper bound for the perimeter of the badge

  b the lower bound for the area of the badge.

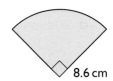

8.6 cm

Number Strand 3 Accuracy
Unit 8 Upper and lower bounds in addition and subtraction

PS PRACTISING SKILLS **DF** DEVELOPING FLUENCY **PB** PROBLEM SOLVING **ES** EXAM-STYLE

PS **1** Write down the number that is halfway between:

    a 5 and 6   **b** 6.5 and 6.6

    c 17.67 and 17.68   **d** 2.362 and 2.363

    e 10 and 10.0001

PS **2** Write down the lower bound and the upper bound for these measurements.

    a The length of a pencil is 14 cm to the nearest centimetre.

    b The length of a race is 100 m measured to the nearest centimetre.

    c The weight of a chocolate bar is 75 g to the nearest gram.

    d The weight of a bag of compost is 25 kg to the nearest 100 grams.

    e The capacity of a bottle of milk is 1 litre measured to the nearest 10 ml.

3 Raphael paints pictures. He charges £150 per square metre for every painting he sells. He paints a rectangular picture that has a length of 1.2 m and a width of 80 cm. Both measurements are correct to the nearest centimetre.

Work out the upper and lower bounds of the cost of this picture.

DF **4** The circumference of the Earth around the equator is 24 900 miles
ES correct to the nearest 10 miles.

    a Work out the upper and lower bounds of the diameter of the Earth.

    b What assumption have you made in carrying out this calculation?

DF **5** Rhodri has a ladder that is 10 m long measured correct to the nearest 2 cm. The base of the ladder has to be 3 m measured to the nearest 5 cm from the base of a wall.

Find the upper bound and the lower bound of the height the ladder can reach up the wall.

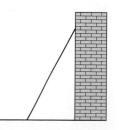

PB
ES
6 Peter cycled to work. His average speed was 4.8 m/s correct to
1 decimal place. It took him 20 minutes correct to the nearest minute.

   a Calculate the lower bound of the distance that Peter travelled
to work.

Peter took a different route home from work. He cycled a distance of 6.2 km
correct to 1 decimal place. It took him 19 minutes correct to the nearest minute.

   b Calculate the upper bound of Peter's average speed in m/s for his
journey home.

PB
ES
7 The average fuel consumption (f) of a car, in kilometres
per litre, is given by the formula $f = \dfrac{d}{u}$ where d is the distance
travelled in kilometres and u is the fuel used in litres.

Jill travels 430 km and uses 52.3 litres of fuel. The 430 is written correct to
3 significant figures. The 52.3 is written correct to one decimal place.

Work out the value of f to a suitable degree of accuracy. You must show
all of your working and give a reason for your final answer.

DF
8 Carys lays 50 squares tiles edge to edge in a straight line.
Each tile has a side of length 5 cm, correct to the nearest 2 mm.

   a What is the least length, in cm, of the straight line of these 50 tiles?

   b What is the greatest length, in cm, of the straight line of these 50 tiles?

PB
9 A bucket holds 5 litres of water, correct to the nearest 0.5 litres.
A tank holds 100 litres, correct to the nearest 4 litres.

How many of these buckets of water would it take to be **certain** to be able to fill
this tank?

You must show all your working.

PB
10 Dafydd cycles 44 km, correct to the nearest 2 km.
It takes him 3 hours, correct to the nearest $\dfrac{1}{2}$ hour.

   a Calculate Dafydd's greatest average speed, in km/hr for this cycle ride.

   b Calculate Dafydd's least average speed, in km/hr for this cycle ride.

Number Strand 5 Percentages
Unit 6 Reverse percentages

PS — PRACTISING SKILLS   DF — DEVELOPING FLUENCY   PB — PROBLEM SOLVING   ES — EXAM-STYLE

PS **1** A washing machine costs £270 which includes VAT at 20%.
Work out the cost of the washing machine without VAT.

PS **2** A computer costs £450 following a reduction of 25%.
Work out the cost of the computer before the reduction.

PS **3** 8717 people visited a tourist attraction in June.
This is a 15% increase in the number of people who visited the attraction in May.
How many people visited the attraction in May?

PS **4** The cost of a barrel of oil at Toby's garage is £45. This is 60% less than
it was 5 years ago.
Work out the cost of a barrel of oil at Toby's garage 5 years ago.

PS **5** A special bottle of Mega Juice contains 1.625 litres of orange juice.
This is 30% more than a standard bottle of Mega Juice.
Work out the amount of orange juice in a standard bottle of Mega Juice.

PS **6** The length of an iron rail at 30°C is 556.2 cm. This is 3% greater than
the length of the iron rail at 10°C.
Work out the length of the iron rail at 10°C.

PS **7** The installation of a contactless ticket machine at a cinema reduces
the average time taken to buy a film ticket by 28%. The average time
taken to buy a film ticket using the contactless ticket machine is 153 seconds.
What was the average time taken to buy a film ticket before the
installation of the contactless ticket machine?

DF **8** A sofa costs £840 which includes VAT at 20%.
Work out the VAT.

DF **9** Work out the original value for each of these.
   a ▢cm is increased by 25% to give 107.5 cm.
   b ▢g is decreased by 5% to give 461.51 g.
   c £▢ is increased by 36.5% to give £352.17.
   d ▢litres is decreased by 17.5% to give 80.85 litres.
   e ▢km is increased by 0.75% to give 39.091 km.

DF 10 Marc buys a suit, a shirt and a tie in a department store sale.

The price of the suit was reduced by 25% to £81.

The price of the shirt was reduced by 20% to £24.

The price of the tie was reduced by 75% to £5.

a What was the price of the suit, the shirt and the tie before the sale?

b How much money did Marc save?

PB ES 11 After a dry summer, Bryn Reservoir contained 1.5×10^{10} litres of water. This is 36% less than the maximum capacity of the reservoir.

Work out the maximum capacity of Bryn Reservoir.

Give your answer in standard form.

PB ES 12 Llinos worked for 20 hours in her part-time job this week.

This was an increase of $33\frac{1}{3}\%$ in the number of hours she worked last week.

a How many hours did Llinos work last week?

b This week Llinos's pay is £144.80. This was more than her pay last week. How much more?

PB ES 13 The handbook of a motorbike states that the pressure, in pounds per square inch (psi), of the back tyre of the motorbike should be:

- in the range 40.5–45 psi

- 12.5% greater than the pressure of the front tyre of the motorbike.

Work out the range of possible pressures for the front tyre of the motorbike.

DF 14 Poppy recorded the times taken by some students to complete a Sudoku puzzle. Here are her results for the male students.

12 min 18 sec   15 min 25 sec   14 min 5 sec   18 min 43 sec   16 min 55 sec

17 min 47 sec   14 min 50 sec   13 min 29 sec   15 min 18 sec   16 min 22 sec

The mean time taken by the male students is 4% less than the mean time taken by the female students.

Work out the mean time taken by the female students.

PB ES 15 There are three heptagons, A, B and C.

The area of C is 30% greater than the area of B.

The area of B is 20% greater than the area of A.

The area of C is 70.2 cm².

Work out the area of A.

PB 16 100 people watched the first round of a darts competition.

122 people watched the second round of the darts competition.

The number of males watching the second round was 20% greater than the number of males watching the first round.

The number of females watching the second round was 25% greater than the number of females watching the first round.

Work out the number of female spectators watching the second round of the competition.

Number Strand 5 Percentages
Unit 7 Repeated percentage increase / decrease

PS PRACTISING SKILLS   **DF** DEVELOPING FLUENCY   **PB** PROBLEM SOLVING   **ES** EXAM-STYLE

PS **1** Write down the meaning of each calculation. The first one has been done for you.

    a 280×1.2 *Increase 280 by 20%.*

    b 280×1.25

    c 280×1.02

    d 280×1.025

    e 280×0.8

PS **2** Copy and complete the calculation to work out each percentage change.

    a Increase 34.5 by 10%. $34.5 \times \boxed{}$

    b Decrease 304 by 12%. $304 \times \boxed{}$

    c Decrease 3.125 by 12.5%. $3.125 \times \boxed{}$

    d Decrease 0.758 by 6.5%. $0.758 \times \boxed{}$

PS **3** Calculate each of these.

    a Increase 400 by 10%. Increase the result by 10%.

    b **i** Increase 520 by 10%. Decrease the result by 10%.

       ii Explain why the answer is not 520.

    c Decrease 1200 by 15%. Increase the result by 20%.

PS **4** Ella invests £5000 into a bank account for 3 years. The bank pays compound interest at an annual rate of 5%.

    Which calculation represents the value of the investment after 3 years?

    a $5000 \times (0.05)^3$ **b** $5000 \times 0.05 \times 3$

    c $5000 \times (1.05)^3$ **d** $5000 \times 1.05 \times 3$

DF **5** Here is a number machine.

Input → × 1.15 → × 0.875 → Output

a Copy and complete the table for this number machine.

Input	520	0.8	108.8	2116
Output				

b What does the number machine do to an input number?
Give your answer in terms of percentages.

DF
ES **6** Mair invests £4000 for 3 years. The investment pays compound
interest at an annual rate of 2%.

Harry invests £3800 for 3 years. His investment pays compound interest at an annual rate of 3%.

The total amount of interest that Harry gets for his investment is more than the total amount of interest that Mair gets for her investment.

How much more?

PB
ES **7** In a sale, the price of handbags are reduced by 30%.

Sam buys a handbag in the sale and uses her loyalty card which gives her a further 10% discount on all items.

The original cost of the handbag is £84.

She pays for the handbag with three £20 notes.

How much change should she get?

PB
ES **8** The value of a new car depreciates with time.

At the end of the first year, the value of the car is 20% less than its value at the beginning of the year.

At the end of the second year, the value of the car is 15% less than its value at the beginning of the year.

At the end of the third year, the value of the car is 10% less than its value at the beginning of the year.

The value of a new car is £16450.

Work out the value of the car after three years.

Give your answer to the nearest £100.

PB
ES **9** Clio plants a tree that is 2m in height.

The height of the tree increases by 10% each year.

How many years will it take for the tree to reach a height of 4m?

Number Strand 5
Percentages Unit 8 Growth and decay

| PS | PRACTISING SKILLS | DF | DEVELOPING FLUENCY | PB | PROBLEM SOLVING | ES | EXAM-STYLE |

PS **1** Write the following percentage changes as decimal multipliers.

    a 20% increase

    b 5% decrease

    c 17.5% increase

    d 2.5% decrease

PS **2** Write the following multipliers as percentage increases or decreases.

    a 1.05

    b 0.9

    c 1.025

    d 0.875

    e 2

PS **3** Rafa invests £500 in an account that pays 3.5% compound interest.

    a Work out how much money Rafa had in the account after four years.

    b How many years would it take for the amount in the account to first exceed £1000?

DF **ES** **4** Rachel invests £250 in a bank account for five years. The bank pays compound interest at an annual rate of 4.5% for the first year and 3.0% for each of the other four years.

How much interest did Rachel earn in total in the five years?

DF **ES** **5** Giovanni invests £12000 in a variable rate compound interest account for three years. The interest rates are 2% for the first year and 3.5% for the second year and 5% for the third year.

Work out the value of Giovanni's investment at the end of the three years.

DF **6** Didi bought a car for £10000. It depreciated 15% in the first year she owned the car and 10% in each subsequent year.

  a Find the value of the car at the end of the third year.

  b How many years will it take for the value of Didi's car take to drop below £4500?

PB **7** A cell reproduces by splitting into two every hour.

  There is one cell at the beginning.

  There are two cells after one hour.

  There are four cells after two hours.

  In hour ($n + 1$) there are twice as many cells as in hour n.

  a Find the number of cells after 10 hours. Give your answer as a power of 2.

  After 24 hours three quarters of the cells were removed.

  b How many cells were left? Give your answer as a power of 2.

PB **8** A scientist is studying some rabbits. The rabbits have a disease that kills the rabbits. A colony of 160 of these rabbits was reduced to 90 in two days. The rabbit population is decreasing exponentially.

  Work out how many of the original population of 160 rabbits will still be alive after seven days.

PB **9** Rhiannon is investigating the population growth of mice held in captivity. There were 120 mice at the start of month 1. There were 240 mice at the start of month 3. The population of mice is increasing exponentially.

  Work out how many mice Rhiannon thinks there will be at the start of month 6.

PB **10** Bill has a beehive. The number of bees in his beehive is decreasing. Bill counts the number of bees in his hive at the start of week 4 and week 6. Here are his results:

Week	Number of bees
4	1600
6	1200

Bill assumes that the population of bees is decreasing exponentially.

How many bees were in the hive at the start of week 1?

Number Strand 6 Ratio and proportion Unit 3 Working with proportional quantities

PS – **PRACTISING SKILLS**　　**DF** – **DEVELOPING FLUENCY**　　**PB** – **PROBLEM SOLVING**　　**ES** – **EXAM-STYLE**

PS　**1**　Seven batteries cost a total of £8.75.

    a　How much does 1 battery cost?

    b　How much do 5 batteries cost?

PS　**2**　Eight calculators cost a total of £46.80.

    a　How much do 5 calculators cost?

    b　How much do 13 calculators cost?

PS　**3**　There are 180 packets of crisps in 5 boxes. How many packets of crisps are there in

    a　3 boxes　　　　　　　　　　**b**　8 boxes?

DF　**4**　Here is a recipe to make 12 almond shortbread biscuits. Grandma is going to use this recipe to make 21 biscuits.

    How much does she need of each ingredient?

> **Almond shortbread biscuits**
> (makes 12 biscuits)
> 5oz butter　　　　　8oz flour
> 1oz ground almonds　　3oz caster sugar

DF　**5**　The label on a 0.75 litre bottle of Fruit Squash says it makes 60 drinks. What should the label on a 1.75 litre bottle of Fruit Squash say about the number of drinks it makes?

DF　**6**　Boxes of paperclips come in two sizes and prices.

    a　For the small box of paperclips, work out the cost of 1 paperclip.

    b　Which box is the better value for money? Explain your answer.

Small box

50 paperclips
£1.40

Large box

225 paperclips
£6.75

DF 7 A spring stretches 6.3 cm when a force of 28 newtons (28 N) is applied to it.

    a How much will the spring stretch when a force of 15 N is applied to it?

    The spring stretches 2.7 cm when a force F N is applied to it.

    b Work out the value of F.

PB 8
ES The table gives information about Mani's pay for last week. This week Mani worked 30 hours at a standard rate and 10 hours at a bonus rate.

How much more did he earn this week compared with last week?

	Number of hours worked	Total
Standard rate	35	£273.70
Bonus rate	5	£60.80
		£334.50

PB 9
ES Aabish is going to make some concrete. She has 100 kg of cement, 180 kg of sharp sand, 400 kg of aggregate and an unlimited supply of water.

Work out the greatest amount of concrete Aabish can make.

Materials for concrete	
(makes 0.125 m³)	
Cement	40 kg
Sharp sand	75 kg
Aggregate	150 kg
Water	22 l

PB 10
ES Baked beans come in three sizes of can. The table gives information about these cans.

Which size of can is the better value for money? Explain your answer.

Size of can	Weight of baked beans (grams)	Cost (p)
Small	180	28
Medium	415	64
Large	840	130

PB 11 The height of the Statue of Liberty is 305 feet. The height of St. Paul's Cathedral is 111 metres. (10 feet is approximately 3 metres)

Which is taller, the Statue of Liberty or St. Paul's Cathedral?

Number Strand 6 Ratio and proportion Unit 4 The constant of proportionality (Algebra)

PS PRACTISING SKILLS **DF** DEVELOPING FLUENCY **PB** PROBLEM SOLVING **ES** EXAM-STYLE

PS **1** y is proportional to x.
When $x = 8$, $y = 5$.

    a Write down a formula involving a constant k that connects y and x.

    b Work out the value of y when $x = 12$.

    c Work out the value of x when $y = 16$.

PS **2** The graph shows information about the variables P and w.

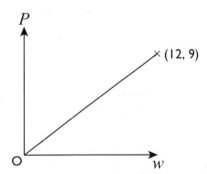

Write down a formula connecting P and w.

PS **3** V is directly proportional to n. The constant of proportionality is 2.25.
Copy and complete the table of values.

n	3	5		12	
V	6.75		15.75		72

PS **4** S is directly proportional to T. When $T = 10$, $S = 120$.

    a Draw the graph of S for $0 \leqslant T \leqslant 10$.

    b Write down a formula connecting S and T.

DF **5** Graham records the values of a variable c for different values of a second variable h.
The table shows his results.

h	2	6	15
c	3	8	20

Graham says, 'c is directly proportional to h'.
Is Graham correct? Give a reason for your answer.

DF **6** The circumference (C) of a circle is directly proportional to its diameter (d).
The graph shows the relationship between C and d.

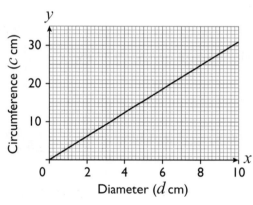

$C = kd$

a Use the graph to find the approximate value of the constant of proportionality k.

b What does the value of k represent in this case?

DF **7** $A = kx$
When $x = 16, A = 4$.

a Work out the value of k.

$B = 1.5x$ and $Y = A + B$

b Copy and complete the table of values for $x = 4, x = 8, x = 12$ and $x = 16$.

x	4	8	12	16
A		2		4
B	6			24
$Y = A + B$	7			28

c Explain why Y is directly proportional to x.

d Write down a formula connecting Y and x.

PB
ES

8 K (kilometres) α M (miles)

16 kilometres = 10 miles

a Write a formula connecting K and M.

b Michael walks 19 kilometres. Sarah walks 12 miles.
Who walked the greater distance, and by how much?

PB

9 The cost of waxing a floor, £C, is directly proportional to the area, a m²,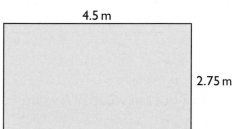
of the floor.

Tracey waxes the floor in her living room. It cost her £350 to wax an area of
28 m².

a Write a formula connecting
C and a.

b What does the value of the constant
of proportionality represent in your
formula?

c The diagram shows the floor plan for
Tracey's dining room.

She has saved £150. Will this be enough
to wax her dining room floor?

4.5 m

2.75 m

PB

10 Larry drives his van at a constant speed.
At this constant speed:

- the cost of fuel, £C, is directly proportional to the distance travelled, d km

- the distance travelled, d km, is directly proportional to the length of time,
t hours, Larry is travelling.

When d = 47.5 km, C = £2.85.

When t = 4.8 hours, d = 210 km.

a Write down a formula connecting

i C and d

ii d and t.

b Work out the value of C when t = 1.6 hours.

c Work out the value of t when C = £50.

Number Strand 6 Ratio and proportion Unit 5 Working with inversely proportional quantities (Algebra)

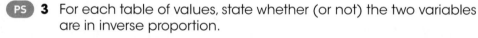

| PS | PRACTISING SKILLS | DF | DEVELOPING FLUENCY | PB | PROBLEM SOLVING | ES | EXAM-STYLE |

PS **1** $h = \dfrac{225}{p}$

Work out the value of h when

a $p = 9$

b $p = 45$.

PS **2** $PV = k$, where k is a constant.
When $V = 10$, $P = 9$.

a Work out the value of k.

b Work out the value of P when $V = 5$.

c Work out the value of V when $P = 15$.

PS **3** For each table of values, state whether (or not) the two variables are in inverse proportion.

a

x	45	60	90	180
y	8	6	4	2

b

x	6	10	15	42
P	35	21	14	5

c

t	2	3	5	7
S	26	39	65	91

d

V	3	15	65	273
R	455	91	21	5

DF **4** $y = \dfrac{k}{x}$, where k is a constant.

    a Copy and complete these statements.

      i y is _____ proportional to _____.

      ii k is the _____.

    b When $x = 5$, $y = 20$.
      Work out the value of k.

    c Work out the value of y when $x = 12.5$.

    d Work out the value of x when $y = 25$.

DF **5** The graph shows V against x.

    a Copy the table and complete
      it using the information in the graph.

x	1	2			6	10
V	30		10	5		

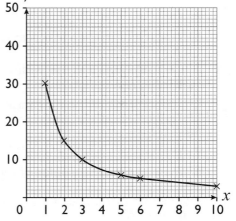

    b Explain why V is inversely proportional to x.

    c Write down a formula connecting V and x.

    d Work out the value of V when

      i $x = 4$

      ii $x = 100$.

    e Work out the value of x when

      i $V = 45$

      ii $V = 150$.

DF **6** For a constant mass of metal, the density, $d\,\mathrm{g/cm^3}$, is inversely
proportional to the volume, $V\,\mathrm{cm^3}$.

The table gives information about the densities and the volumes of 1 kg of some
common metals. All measurements are correct to 3 significant figures.

Metal	Gold	Silver	Lead	Copper	Iron	Platinum
Density $d\,\mathrm{g/cm^3}$	19.3	10.5	11.3	8.96	7.87	21.5
Volume, $V\,\mathrm{cm^3}$	51.8	95.2	88.5	112.0	127.0	46.5

    a Draw a graph of V against d.

    b Write down a formula connecting V and d for 1 kg of a metal.

    c The density of mercury is $13.5\,\mathrm{g/cm^3}$. Work out the volume of 1 kg of mercury.

DF **7** The volume (V) of a gas is inversely proportional to the pressure (P) at constant temperature.

There is 10000 cm³ of neon gas in a balloon at a pressure of 1.5 atmospheres.

Work out the volume of neon gas in the balloon when the pressure is increased to 2 atmospheres. Assume the temperature is constant.

PB **8** The cost of the labour to build a patio is £600.

ES The table gives some information about the hourly rate, £R, and the time taken, t hours, to build the patio.

t	25	40	50	60	75
R	24	15	12	10	8

a Write down a formula connecting R and t.

b Work out the hourly rate when it takes 30 hours to build the patio.

c Work out the time taken to build the patio for an hourly rate of £12.50.

PB **9** The length, y m, and the width, x m, of the rectangle are variables.

ES The area, A m², of the rectangle is a constant.

$A = 3990$

a Write down a formula connecting y and x.

b Work out the perimeter of the rectangle when

  i $x = 38$

  ii $y = 76$.

A m² x m

y m

PB **10** Kerry is putting some washers into bags. She puts the same number of washers into each bag.

ES The number of washers, w, she puts into each bag is inversely proportional to the number of bags, p, she uses.

a Copy and complete the table of values.

Number of washers in each bag, w	15	30		45
Number of bags, p	42		18	

b How many of these washers can Kerry put into each of 105 bags?

c Kerry puts 21 of these washers into each bag. A bag costs 5p.
Work out the total cost of the bags.

Number Strand 6 Ratio and proportion Unit 6 Formulating equations to solve proportion problems (Algebra)

PS – PRACTISING SKILLS   **DF** – DEVELOPING FLUENCY   **PB** – PROBLEM SOLVING   **ES** – EXAM-STYLE

PS **1** Write the following relationships using the 'proportional to' sign ($\propto$).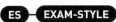

   a y varies as x

   b y varies as the square of x

   c y varies inversely as x

   d y varies as the square root of x

   e y varies as the cube of x

   f y varies inversely as the square of x

PS **2** Given that $y = 40$ when $x = 10$, write an equation to show each of these relationships.

   a y varies as x

   b y varies as the square of x

   c y varies inversely as x

   d y varies as the square root of x

   e y varies as the cube of x

   f y varies inversely as the square of x

PS **ES** **3** p varies as the square of t. When $p = 75$, $t = 5$. Find the value of p when $t = 8$.

PS **ES** **4** r varies inversely as the cube of s. When $r = 5$, $s = 2$. Find the value of r when $s = \frac{1}{2}$.

DF **ES** **5** The time taken for the pendulum of a clock to make one complete swing is proportional to the square root of the length of the pendulum.

When the pendulum is 50 cm long the time for one complete swing is one second.

How long is the pendulum when one complete swing takes two seconds?

DF **ES** **6** Delyth carries out an experiment on how long a liquid takes to cool in a freezer.

She records the time (m) in minutes and temperature (t) in degrees Celsius. Here are her results:

Time m	1	4	9	x
Temperature t	24	12	8	4.8

Delyth thinks that t varies inversely as the square root of m.

Find the value of x when the temperature is 4.8°C.

PB **ES** **7** The resistance to motion of a car is directly proportional the square of the speed of the car. When the speed of the car is 25 metres per second the resistance to motion is 80 000 N.

Find the resistance to motion when the speed of the car is 108 km per hour.

PB **ES** **8** In the winter a farmer feeds his cattle with hay each day. The number of days, d, the hay will last is inversely proportional to the number of cows, c. The farmer has enough hay to feed 120 cows for 30 days. The farmer has a herd of 75 cows.

For how many days will the farmer be able to feed his cows?

PB **ES** **9** Aled plays in a band. The loudness of the music varies inversely as the square of the distance from the band. Aled measures the loudness of his band as 115 decibels at a distance of 4 m.

Aled's band are playing at a wedding. They have to stop playing if the loudness is more than 100 decibels at a distance of 5 m.

Explain if Aled's band have to stop playing.

PB **ES** **10** The pressure, P, on a diver as she dives under the water is proportional to the square of her depth, d, below the surface of the water. She dives to 10 m below the surface of the water.

Explain why she needs to dive a further $10(\sqrt{2} - 1)$ m for the pressure to double.

Number Strand 7 Number properties Unit 6 Rules of indices

PS—**PRACTISING SKILLS** **DF**—**DEVELOPING FLUENCY** **PB**—**PROBLEM SOLVING** **ES**—**EXAM-STYLE**

PS **1** Copy and complete the table by writing each number as a single power of 5.

Ordinary number	125	25	5	1	$\frac{1}{5}$	$\frac{1}{25}$	$\frac{1}{125}$
Index form		5^2					

PS **2** Use the rule $a^n \times a^m = a^{n+m}$ to simplify each of these. Give your answers in index form.

   a $2^3 \times 2^4$

   b $2^{-1} \times 2^5$

   c $7^3 \times 7^0$

PS **3** Use the rule $a^n \div a^m = a^{n-m}$ to simplify each of these. Give your answers in index form.

   a $5^7 \div 5^6$

   b $7^{-1} \div 7^{-1}$

   c $\dfrac{11^{-2}}{11^8}$

PS **4** Use the rule $(a^m)^n = a^{m \times n}$ to simplify each of these. Give your answers in index form.

   a $(5^2)^3$

   b $(2^5)^0$

   c $(11^{-3})^{-2}$

PS **5** Write each of these as a fraction in its simplest form.

For example, $2^{-3} = \dfrac{1}{2^3} = \dfrac{1}{8}$.

   a 2^{-2} **b** 3^{-2} **c** 11^{-1} **d** 10^{-3}

DF **6** Without using a calculator, state which of these is equal to 1.

   a 5^0 **b** $3^2 \times 3^{-2}$ **c** $(5^3)^{-2}$ **d** $2^5 \div 2^5$ **e** $(7^3)^0$

DF **7** Write each of these as a single power of 2.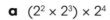

     a 4   **b** 4^2 **c** $(4^3)^2$ **d** $(4^5)^4$

DF **8** Work out each of these. Give your answers in index form.

     a $(2^2 \times 2^3) \times 2^4$

     b $(7^3 \times 7^4) \div 7^5$

     c $(2^3)^2 \times (2^2)^3$

     d $(5^4 \div 5^6)^{-1}$

DF **9** $3^4 = 81$ and $3^5 = 243$

     Write the answer to each of these as a single power of 3. Do not use a calculator.

     a 9×81

     b $\dfrac{243}{9}$

     c $\dfrac{243 \times 81^2}{27}$

DF **10** Use the rules of indices to simplify each of these. Give your answers in index form.

     a $2^3 \times 2^4 \times 3^4 \times 3^2$

     b $\dfrac{3^5 \times 5^4}{3^2 \times 5^2}$

     c $(2^5 \times 5^3)^2$

DF **11** Without using a calculator, copy and complete these statements.
Use < or > or =.

     a 2^3 ☐ 3^2

     b 2^{-1} ☐ 3^{-1}

     c 3^0 ☐ 3

PB **12** $5^3 = 125$ and $5^5 = 3125$

ES   Pierre says $125^{10} = 3125^6$.

     Without using a calculator, say whether or not he is correct. Explain why.

PB **13** Aled says $(a^m)^n = (a^n)^m$.

ES   Is he correct? Explain why.

PB **14** Write down the HCF of each pair of numbers.

ES   **a** 42 and 70

     b 42^2 and 70^2

Number Strand 7 Number properties Unit 7 Fractional indices

PS — **PRACTISING SKILLS** **DF** — **DEVELOPING FLUENCY** **PB** — **PROBLEM SOLVING** **ES** — **EXAM-STYLE**

PS **1** Write the following as roots.

  a $5^{\frac{1}{2}}$ **b** $4^{\frac{1}{3}}$ **c** $3^{\frac{1}{4}}$

  d $8^{\frac{1}{2}}$ **e** $10^{\frac{1}{5}}$ **f** $6^{\frac{1}{5}}$

PS **2** Write the following using indices.

  a $\sqrt{7}$ **b** $\sqrt[3]{9}$ **c** $\sqrt[3]{4}$

  d $\sqrt{5}$ **e** $\sqrt[6]{5}$ **f** $\sqrt[7]{2}$

PS **3** Find the value of each of these.

  a $81^{\frac{1}{2}}$ **b** $8^{\frac{1}{3}}$ **c** $256^{\frac{1}{4}}$

  d $169^{\frac{1}{2}}$ **e** $216^{\frac{1}{3}}$ **f** $625^{\frac{1}{4}}$

DF **4** Write the following using roots.

  a $5^{\frac{3}{2}}$ **b** $7^{\frac{2}{3}}$ **c** $6^{\frac{3}{4}}$

  d $10^{\frac{5}{3}}$ **e** $10^{\frac{2}{5}}$ **f** $5^{\frac{5}{2}}$

DF **5** Write the following using indices.

  a $\sqrt{2^3}$ **b** $(\sqrt[4]{3})^3$ **c** $\sqrt[3]{5^7}$

  d $\sqrt[4]{7^5}$ **e** $(\sqrt[3]{2})^5$ **f** $(\sqrt[5]{2})^9$

DF **6** Find the value of each of these.

  a $36^{\frac{3}{2}}$ **b** $8^{\frac{2}{3}}$ **c** $256^{\frac{3}{4}}$

  d $4^{\frac{5}{2}}$ **e** $27^{\frac{5}{3}}$ **f** $625^{\frac{3}{4}}$

DF **7** Write the following as roots.

  a $3^{-\frac{1}{2}}$ **b** $4^{-\frac{1}{3}}$ **c** $5^{-\frac{3}{4}}$

  d $7^{-\frac{3}{2}}$ **e** $9^{-\frac{4}{5}}$ **f** $3^{-\frac{2}{5}}$

DF **8** Write the following using indices.

a $\dfrac{1}{\sqrt{5}}$ b $\dfrac{1}{\sqrt[4]{7}}$ c $\dfrac{1}{\sqrt[3]{5^2}}$

d $\dfrac{1}{(\sqrt{7})^3}$ e $\dfrac{1}{\sqrt[4]{3^5}}$ f $\dfrac{1}{(\sqrt[5]{3})^3}$

DF **9** Find the value of each of these.

a $16^{-\frac{3}{2}}$ b $64^{-\frac{2}{3}}$ c $125^{-\frac{5}{3}}$

d $4^{-\frac{3}{2}}$ e $27^{-\frac{2}{3}}$ f $64^{-\frac{5}{6}}$

PB **10** Write the value of each of these as a power of 2.

a $4 \times 32^{\frac{3}{5}}$

b $\dfrac{1}{8} \times 64^{\frac{3}{2}}$

c $8^{-\frac{5}{3}} \times 32^{\frac{2}{5}}$

PB **11** Find the value of n.

a $\dfrac{1}{\sqrt{8}} = 2^n$

b $\sqrt[3]{27^2} = 3^n$

c $(\sqrt[3]{125})^4 = 25^n$

PB **12** a Work out $\left(\dfrac{125}{27}\right)^{-\frac{2}{3}}$

ES b Find the value of p in this numeric identity.

$3 \times 8^{\frac{2}{3}} = 96 \times p^{-\frac{1}{3}}$

Number Strand 7 Number properties Unit 8 Surds

PS PRACTISING SKILLS **DF** DEVELOPING FLUENCY **PB** PROBLEM SOLVING **ES** EXAM-STYLE

PS 1 Write the following roots in the form $a\sqrt{b}$.

    a $\sqrt{8}$ **b** $\sqrt{27}$ **c** $\sqrt{20}$ **d** $\sqrt{200}$ **e** $\sqrt{72}$ **f** $\sqrt{63}$

PS 2 Simplify the following roots.

    a $\sqrt{48}$ **b** $\sqrt{18}$ **c** $\sqrt{54}$ **d** $\sqrt{500}$ **e** $\sqrt{45}$ **f** $\sqrt{125}$

PS 3 Rationalise the denominator of each of these fractions.

    a $\dfrac{3}{\sqrt{2}}$ **b** $\dfrac{3}{\sqrt{3}}$ **c** $\dfrac{4}{\sqrt{5}}$ **d** $\dfrac{20}{\sqrt{10}}$ **e** $\dfrac{3}{\sqrt{6}}$ **f** $\dfrac{15}{\sqrt{10}}$

DF 4 Write each of the following fractions in its simplest form.

    a $\dfrac{2}{\sqrt{2}}$ **b** $\dfrac{25}{\sqrt{5}}$ **c** $\dfrac{4\sqrt{3}}{\sqrt{12}}$ **d** $\dfrac{25}{\sqrt{10}}$ **e** $\dfrac{3\sqrt{2}}{\sqrt{8}}$ **f** $\dfrac{3\sqrt{5}}{\sqrt{10}}$

DF 5 Multiply out and simplify the bracketed expressions.

    a $(3+\sqrt{2})(3-\sqrt{2})$ **b** $(3+\sqrt{2})(3+\sqrt{2})$

    c $(\sqrt{3}+\sqrt{2})(\sqrt{3}-\sqrt{2})$ **d** $(\sqrt{3}-\sqrt{2})(\sqrt{3}-\sqrt{2})$

    e $(\sqrt{3}+\sqrt{2})^2$ **f** $(\sqrt{75}+\sqrt{72})(\sqrt{75}-\sqrt{72})$

DF 6 Rationalise the denominator and write the answer as a surd in its simplest form.

    a $\dfrac{1}{5+\sqrt{7}}$ **b** $\dfrac{4}{5-\sqrt{7}}$ **c** $\dfrac{\sqrt{7}}{5+\sqrt{7}}$

    d $\dfrac{1}{\sqrt{7}+\sqrt{5}}$ **e** $\dfrac{\sqrt{35}}{\sqrt{7}-\sqrt{5}}$

PB **ES** **7** Explain why the angle marked x is 60°.

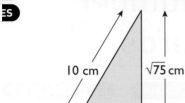

10 cm $\sqrt{75}$ cm

x

PB **ES** **8** Explain why the angle marked y is 30°.

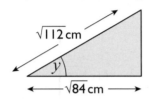

$\sqrt{112}$ cm

y

$\sqrt{84}$ cm

PB **ES** **9** Squares are drawn on the sides of the right-angled triangle. Work out the perimeter of the right-angled triangle. Give your answer in surd form.

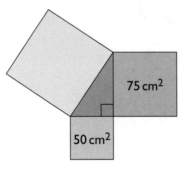

75 cm²

50 cm²

PB **ES** **10** PQR is a right-angled triangle. All the measurements are in cm.

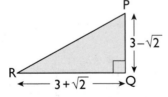

P

$3-\sqrt{2}$

R

$3+\sqrt{2}$

Q

a Work out the area of triangle PQR.

b Work out the perimeter of triangle PQR.

Algebra Strand 1 Starting algebra Unit 9 Simplifying harder expressions

PS – PRACTISING SKILLS   DF – DEVELOPING FLUENCY   PB – PROBLEM SOLVING   ES – EXAM-STYLE

PB
ES
1 Waqar, Nathan and Wesley play for the school football team.

Waqar has scored 5 more goals than Nathan.

If Nathan scores another goal, he will have scored twice as many goals as Wesley.

Wesley has scored g goals. The three boys have scored a total of T goals.

Write down an expression for T in terms of g.

PB
2 Tom thinks of a number n and adds 4.

Jane thinks of a number m and subtracts 7.

Write down and expand an expression for the product of their results.

PB
ES
3 Write down an expression, in terms of x, for the area of this shape.

$(2x - 1)$ cm

$(x + 1)$ cm

$(2x - 1)$ cm

$(x + 1)$ cm

PB
ES
4 The diagram shows a lawn in the shape of a square with a path around it.

The lawn is of side $(x + 3)$ m.

The width of the path is 1 m.

Write down an expression, in terms of x, for the total area of the path.

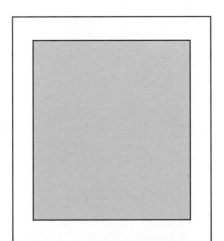

5 The diagram shows a square and a right-angled triangle.

Show that the area of the square is never equal to the area of the right-angled triangle.

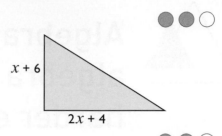

6 Show that the area of this trapezium is $x^2 - 16$.

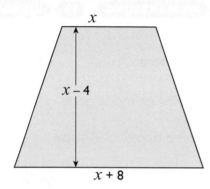

7 Write down in terms of x

a the area of the shaded rectangle

b the area of the shaded triangle.

Expand and simplify your expressions, if necessary.

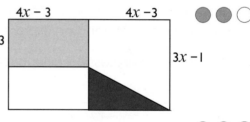

8 Here is a right-angled triangle.

Write down an expression for y in terms of x.

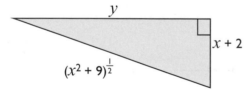

9 a Expand and simplify $(y - 5)(y + 8)$.

b Simplify $\dfrac{(2w^2x)^3}{2w^3x \times 3wx^2}$.

10 $\left(x^{n+1}\right)^{n-1} = x^3$

For what value of n is this statement true?

Algebra Strand 1 Starting algebra Unit 10 Using complex formulae

PS — **PRACTISING SKILLS**   **DF** — **DEVELOPING FLUENCY**   **PB** — **PROBLEM SOLVING**   **ES** — **EXAM-STYLE**

PB
ES
1 BB Cars uses the formula $C = 20 + 12.5Gt$ to work out the cost, £C, of renting a car, where G is the group of the car (1, 2, 3 or 4) and t is the number of days for which the car is rented.

Mary paid £370 to rent a car from BB Cars.

Work out one possibility for the number of days and the group of car that Mary rented.

PS
ES
2 Here is a formula.

$v = u + at$

a Work out the value of v when $u = 25$, $a = -10$ and $t = 3.5$.

b Rearrange the formula to make a the subject.

c Work out the value of a when $v = 80$, $u = 60$ and $t = 15$.

DF
ES
3 The formula for calculating the volume (V) of a sphere is $V = \frac{4}{3}\pi r^3$, where r is the radius of the sphere.

a Work out the volume of a sphere of radius 4.5 cm. Leave your answer in terms of π.

b Work out the radius of a sphere of volume 200 mm³. Take $\pi = 3.14$.

PB
ES
4 A can of cola is in the shape of a cylinder.

The volume of a cylinder (V) is given by the formula $V = \pi r^2 h$, where r is the radius and h is the height of the cylinder.

Peter buys a can that holds 330 ml of cola.

The radius of the can is 3.25 cm.

Work out the height of the can. Take $\pi = 3.14$.

DF
ES
5 The surface area (A) of a solid cylinder can be found using the formula $A = 2\pi r^2 + 2\pi rh$, where r is the radius of the cylinder and h is its height.

a Work out the surface area of a cylinder with radius 7 cm and height 15 cm. Give your answer in terms of π.

b Work out the height of a cylinder with surface area 20π and radius 2 cm.

PS
ES
6 Here is a formula.

$v^2 = u^2 + 2as$

  a Work out the value of v when $u = 20$, $a = 10$ and $s = 11.25$.

  b Rearrange the formula to make u the subject.

  c Work out the value of u when $v = 9$, $a = 4$ and $s = 7$.

PB
ES
7 To change P pounds into E euros, Pete uses the formula $E = 1.36P$.
To change P pounds into D dollars, Pete uses the formula $D = 1.55P$.

  a Write down a formula that Pete could use to change dollars into euros.

  b Pete sees a watch for sale on an American website for 200 dollars.
  The same model of watch is for sale in Spain for 175 euros.
  In the UK, this model of watch is sold for 130 pounds.
  In which currency is the watch cheapest?

DF
ES
8 The formula $T = 2\pi\sqrt{\dfrac{l}{g}}$ is used to calculate the time period, T, of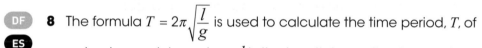

a simple pendulum where l is the length in centimetres and g is the acceleration due to gravity.

  a Work out the value of T when $l = 160\,\text{cm}$ and $g = 10\,\text{m/s}^2$.
  Give your answer in terms of π.

  b For another simple pendulum, $T = \dfrac{2\pi}{7}$.
  Work out the length of this simple pendulum when $g = 9.8\,\text{m/s}^2$.

PS
ES
9 Here is a formula.

$c = \sqrt{a^2 + b^2}$

  a Make b the subject of the formula.

  b Work out the value of b when $c = 41$ and $a = 40$.

PS
ES
10 Here is a formula.

$E = mc^2$

Work out the value of

  a E when $m = 2 \times 10^{30}$ and $c = 3 \times 10^8$

  b m when $E = 4.5 \times 10^{28}$ and $c = 3 \times 10^8$.

Algebra Strand 1 Starting algebra Unit 11 Identities

PS ─ PRACTISING SKILLS   **DF** ─ DEVELOPING FLUENCY   **PB** ─ PROBLEM SOLVING   **ES** ─ EXAM-STYLE

PS **1** Write down whether each statement is an identity (I), an equation (Q), an expression (X) or a formula (F).

    a $m^2 + 5m + 6 = 0$

    b $m^2 + 5m + 6$

    c $m^2 + 5m + 6 = (m + 3)(m + 2)$

    d $f = m^2 + 5m + 6$

    e $m^2 + 5m + 6 = m(m + 5) + 6$

DF **2** Which of the following are not identities?

    A $1 - 2(a - 1) = -2a - 1$ **B** $1 - 2(a - 1) = -2a + 3$

    C $1 - 2(a - 1) = 1 - 2a - 2$ **D** $1 - 2(a - 1) = 1 - 2a + 2$

    E $1 - 2(a - 1) = 1 + 2a + 2$

DF **3** **a** Write down one value of x for which the statement $(x + 4)^2 = x^2 + 4^2$ is true.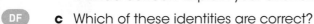

PB   **b** Linda says that $(x + 4)^2 = x^2 + 4^2$ is true for all values of x.

       Is Linda correct? Explain your answer.

DF   **c** Which of these identities are correct?

       A $(x + 4)^2 \equiv x^2 + 4^2$ **B** $(x + 4)^2 \equiv x^2 + 4x + 16$ **C** $(x + 4)^2 \equiv x^2 + 8x + 16$

       D $(x + 4)^2 \equiv x^2 + 4x + 8$ **E** $(x + 4)^2 \equiv x^2 + 8x + 8$

PB **4** Dave is three times older than Anne.
ES   Julie is 5 years older than Anne.

    Julie is twice as old as Colin.

    Anne is x years old.

    a Write down an expression, in terms of x, for the sum of their ages.

    b Write down the integer values of x, for which

       i Dave is the oldest of the four

       ii Julie is the oldest of the four.

DF **5** $x^2 - 4x - 9$ can be written in the form $(x - 2)^2 + k$.
ES   **a** Work out the value of k.

    b Solve the equation $x^2 - 4x - 9 = 0$.

DF
ES

6 Work out the values of a, b and c if
$(x + 5)^2 + (x - 4)^2 = ax^2 + bx + c$.

PB
ES

7 a Show that the area of this shape is $9y^2 + 2y - 24$.

   b Leo says the area is 24 cm².
   Explain why this is not true.

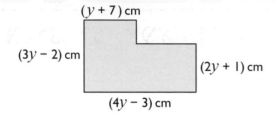

(y + 7) cm

(3y − 2) cm

(2y + 1) cm

(4y − 3) cm

DF
ES

8 Show that

   a $\dfrac{x + 1}{3} - \dfrac{x - 1}{2} = \dfrac{5 - x}{6}$

   b $\dfrac{1}{1 - x} + \dfrac{1}{1 + x} = \dfrac{2}{1 - x^2}$

DF
ES

9 Prove that

   a The sum of any two odd numbers is always even.

   b The sum of the squares of two consecutive numbers is always odd.

   c The difference between the squares of any two odd numbers is always even.

PB
ES

10 Explain why the area of this triangle can never be a whole number of cm² when x is an odd number.

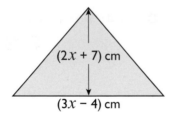

(2x + 7) cm

(3x − 4) cm

Algebra Strand 1 Starting algebra Unit 12 Using indices in algebra

PS — PRACTISING SKILLS   **DF** — DEVELOPING FLUENCY   **PB** — PROBLEM SOLVING   **ES** — EXAM-STYLE

PS **ES** **1** Here is an input–output machine.

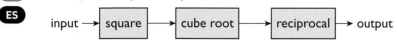

input → □ square □ → □ cube root □ → □ reciprocal □ → output

     a   Work out the output, as a power of c, when the input is c.

     b   Work out the input, as a power of d, when the output is d.

PS **2** Simplify these.

     a $(a^2b^3)^{-1} \div ab^2$

     b $\sqrt{ab^{-1}} \times \dfrac{1}{\sqrt{a^3b}}$

     c $\dfrac{p^3}{q^2} \div \dfrac{q^{-1}}{\sqrt{p}}$

     d $\dfrac{\sqrt[3]{p^2}}{q^{-2}} \times \dfrac{(2q)^2}{p^4}$

DF **ES** **3** Simplify these.

     a $(2pq^2)^2 \div (4p^3(q^2)^{-1})$

     b $\sqrt{(2pq)^3 \times 2pq^{-5}}$

     c $\dfrac{a^2b^{\frac{1}{3}} \times a^{-1}b^{\frac{2}{3}}}{ab}$

     d $\sqrt[3]{\dfrac{p^2q \times p^5q^3}{pq}}$

PB **ES** **4** The area of this square is the same as the area of this right-angled triangle.

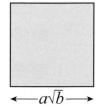
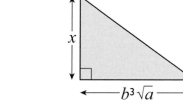

x can be written in the form pa^nb^m.

Find the values of p, n and m.

DF **ES** **5** $x = a^2b^{-\frac{3}{2}}$ $y = a^{\frac{5}{2}}b^2$

    a Work out the square of xy.

    b Work out the cube of $\dfrac{x}{y}$.

PS **6** Write each of the following as a power of x.

    a $\dfrac{x}{\sqrt{4x^4}}$ **b** $((x^2)^{-5})^{-1}$ **c** $\sqrt[3]{x^{-4}}$

    d $\dfrac{1}{\sqrt{x^3}}$ **e** $\left(\dfrac{x^2}{x^{-3}}\right)^{\frac{1}{2}}$ **f** $\dfrac{\sqrt[3]{x}}{(2x^{-1})^3}$

DF **ES** **7** Find the value of n in the following equations.

    a $\sqrt{p} \times p^n = \dfrac{1}{p}$

    b $\dfrac{q^3}{\sqrt{q} \times q^n} = q^{\frac{5}{2}}$

DF **ES** **8** **a** Simplify $(\sqrt{a} - 3\sqrt{b})(2\sqrt{a} + \sqrt{b})$.

    b Write as a single fraction $\dfrac{2}{\sqrt{n}} + \dfrac{3\sqrt{n}}{4}$.

    c Solve $5^x = \dfrac{1}{125}$.

PB **ES** **9** The area of this right-angled triangle is $15\,\text{cm}^2$.

    a Show that the area of this right-angled triangle can be written as $2\sqrt{a^5b^3}$.

    b Find an expression, in terms of a and b, for the length of the hypotenuse.

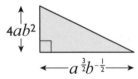

$4ab^2$

$a^{\frac{3}{2}}b^{-\frac{1}{2}}$

DF **ES** **10** **a** Simplify $2a^3b^{-1} \times \dfrac{5}{ab^2}$.

    b $x^{2.5} \times x^{n-1} = \dfrac{1}{\sqrt{x}}$. Work out the value of n.

Algebra Strand 1 Starting algebra Unit 13 Manipulating more expressions and equations

PS PRACTISING SKILLS   **DF** DEVELOPING FLUENCY   **PB** PROBLEM SOLVING   **ES** EXAM-STYLE

PS **1** Expand and simplify these.

    a $(x + 7)(x + 9)$

    b $(x - 5)(x + 11)$

    c $(x - 4)(x - 5)$

    d $(2x + 3)(5x - 2)$

    e $(3 - x)(5 + 2x)$

    f $(x - 6)(7 - 2x)$

PB **2** $(3x + 1)(ax + b) = 6x^2 - 7x - 3$

ES   Work out the values and a and b.

DF **3** **a** Expand $(x - 1)(x - 2)(x - 3)$

ES   **b** $(x + 3)(x - a)(x - b) = x^3 + 2x^2 - 23x - 60$. Work out the values
      of a and b.

PB **4** It takes Asif 15 minutes more than Waqar to travel a distance

ES   of 20 miles. It takes Waqar t hours to travel this distance of 20 miles.

   Work out the difference, in terms of t, in their average speeds.

DF **5** Solve these.

ES   **a** $\dfrac{x}{4} + \dfrac{x}{5} = 1$

   b $\dfrac{x-1}{2} - \dfrac{x+1}{3} = 6$

PB **6** The area of this right-angled triangle is $15\,\text{cm}^2$. Work out the

ES   perimeter of the triangle.

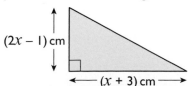

PS **7** Expand and simplify these.

    a $(\sqrt{x} - 1)(\sqrt{x} + 1)$

    b $(x - \sqrt{3})(x + 2\sqrt{3})$

    c $(\sqrt{x} + \sqrt{5})(\sqrt{x} + \sqrt{10})$

    d $(2\sqrt{x} + \sqrt{3})^2$

DF **8** Simplify these.

ES

    a $\dfrac{(6a - 2b)}{(2a + b)(3a - b)}$

    b $\dfrac{p^2 - pq - 2q^2}{p^2 - q^2}$

DF **9** Simplify these.

ES

    a $\dfrac{(u + v)^2 - w^2}{(w + v)^2 - u^2}$

    b $\dfrac{b^2 - ac - ab - bc}{c^2 - ac + ab - bc}$

DF **10** Write the following as powers of x.

    a $10\left(x + \dfrac{1}{x}\right) = 29$

    b $\dfrac{10x + 1}{2x - 1} - \dfrac{3x + 8}{x + 1} = 2$

PB **11** The diagram shows a net of an open metal box. The net is cut

ES from a sheet of dimensions $(x + 2)$ cm by $(x - 1)$ cm. A square of side 1 cm is cut out at each corner. The net is then folded along the dotted lines to form the box.

If the volume of the box is 70 cm³, work out the dimensions of the sheet of metal.

DF **12** $x = 1 + \dfrac{p}{p - q}$ $y = 2 - \dfrac{3q}{p + q}$. Find

ES

    a $\dfrac{x}{y}$

    b $\dfrac{3}{x} + \dfrac{1}{y}$

Algebra Strand 1 Starting algebra Unit 14 Rearranging more formulae

PS – PRACTISING SKILLS   **DF** – DEVELOPING FLUENCY   **PB** – PROBLEM SOLVING   **ES** – EXAM-STYLE

PS **1** Make the letter shown in brackets the subject of each formula.

    a $b = a + (n - 1)d$ (n) **b** $e = \frac{1}{2}mc^2$ (c)

    c $t = w\sqrt{ag}$ (g) **d** $s = ut + \frac{1}{2}at^2$ (a)

PS **ES** **2** Here is a prism. The cross section is in the shape of a trapezium.

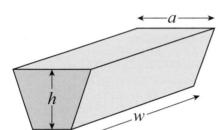

The volume, V, of the prism is given by the formula $V = \frac{w}{2}(a + b)h$ where h is the height, w is the length, and a and b are the widths of the top and bottom of the trapezium.

    a Make b the subject of the formula.

    b Find b when $V = 450$, $a = 12$, $h = 5$ and $w = 10$.

DF **ES** **3** Make a the subject of the formula $\cos A = \dfrac{b^2 + c^2 - a^2}{2bc}$.

DF **ES** **4** The curved surface area, A, of a cone is given by the formula $A = \pi r\sqrt{h^2 + r^2}$ where h is the height and r is the radius of the cone.

    a Make h the subject of the formula.

    b Find h when $A = 550$ and $r = 10$. Take $\pi = 3.14$. Give your answer to three significant figures.

DF **5** Make w the subject of the formula $T = w + \dfrac{wv^2}{gx}$.

6 A wire L metres long is stretched between two points. The points are at the same level and are d metres apart. The sag, s metres,

in the middle of the wire is given by the formula $s = \sqrt{\dfrac{3d(L-d)}{8}}$

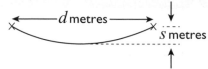

$-d$ metres — s metres

a Rearrange the formula to make L the subject.

b Work out the length of wire that gives a sag of 0.6 m when the two points are 16 m apart.

DF **7** Make k the subject of the formula $T = 2\pi\sqrt{\dfrac{h^2 + k^2}{2gh}}$.

8 The total resistance, R ohms, of two resistors in parallel is given by $\dfrac{1}{R} = \dfrac{1}{x} + \dfrac{1}{y}$ where x and y are the resistances, in ohms, of the two resistors.

a Make y the subject of the formula.

b Find y when $x = 2\dfrac{1}{3}$ ohms and $R = 2\dfrac{1}{4}$ ohms.

DF **9** **a** $x = a + \sqrt{b(x-a)}$. Find x in terms of a and b only.

b Make p the subject of $A = \sqrt{\dfrac{p^2 - 2q^2}{2p^2 + q^2}}$.

DF **10** $E = 2c\left(1 + \dfrac{1}{m}\right)$ and $E = 3k\left(1 - \dfrac{2}{m}\right)$.

Express m in terms of c and k only.

11 An arithmetic sequence is formed by adding d to the previous term. If the first term is a, the sum, S, of the first n terms is given by the formula $S = \dfrac{n}{2}\big[2a + (n-1)d\big]$.

a Make d the subject of this formula.

b 25 is the first term of an arithmetic sequence. The sum of the first 32 terms is 56. Find d.

DF **12** Make d the subject of $A = \sqrt{\dfrac{2v^2d}{g} + \dfrac{d^2}{4}} - \dfrac{d}{2}$.

Algebra Strand 2 Sequences
Unit 4 Special sequences

PS — **PRACTISING SKILLS** **DF** — **DEVELOPING FLUENCY** **PB** — **PROBLEM SOLVING** **ES** — **EXAM-STYLE**

DF **1** Here are the first eight terms of a sequence.

0   2   2   4   6   10   16   26

    a Describe the rule for working out the terms in this sequence.

    b Johan says: 'All the terms in this sequence must be even numbers.'
Explain why Johan is right.

    c What is special about these numbers?

PS
ES **2** Here are the first three patterns in a sequence of patterns.

    a Write down the first 5 terms in the sequence formed by
the vertical lines.

    b Show that the nth term of this sequence can be
written as $\dfrac{n(n+3)}{2}$.

PB
ES **3** Here is a sequence of patterns made with dots and straight lines.

 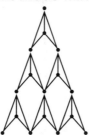

  Pattern 1   Pattern 2   Pattern 3

    a Find the missing numbers in the table.

Pattern number	1	2	3	4	10
Number of dots	4	9			
Number of lines	5	15			
Number of triangles	2	6			

b Write down, in terms of n, the nth term for the sequence of dots.

c i Show that the nth term for the sequence of triangles is $n^2 + n$.

   ii Use $n^2 + n$ to help you write, in terms of n, the nth term for the sequence of lines.

PB **ES** **4** Here are the first three terms of a sequence.

   1   3   7

Alan says the next term in this sequence is 13. Becky says the next term in this sequence is 15.

a Explain how **both** Alan and Becky could be right.

b i Write down the 5th term of Alan's sequence.

   ii Write down the 5th term of Becky's sequence.

PB **ES** **5** Here are the first four terms of a sequence.

   16   8   4   2

a Write down the next three terms of this sequence.

b Which of the following expressions is the nth term of this sequence?

$$\frac{32}{2^{n+1}} \qquad \frac{n}{2} \qquad 2n \qquad \frac{32}{2^{n-1}} \qquad \frac{32}{2^n}$$

PB **ES** **6** P_n is the perimeter of an equilateral triangle. The next equilateral triangle is formed by joining the midpoints of the triangle. This is shown in the diagram.

$P_1 = 3s$

Write down P_2, P_3, P_4 and P_5 in terms of s.

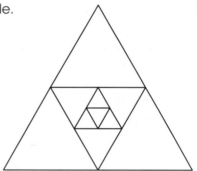

Algebra Strand 2 Sequences
Unit 5 Quadratic sequences

PS — PRACTISING SKILLS   **DF** — DEVELOPING FLUENCY   **PB** — PROBLEM SOLVING   **ES** — EXAM-STYLE

PS **ES** **1** **a** Write down the first four terms of a quadratic sequence with nth term $2n^2 - 6n + 5$.

b Explain why every term of this sequence is an odd number.

PS **ES** **2** Here are the first few terms of a sequence.

0, 4, 18, 48, 100, …

a Explain why this is not a quadratic sequence.

b Find the 10th term.

PB **ES** **3** The nth term of an arithmetic sequence is $2n + 10$.

The nth term of a quadratic sequence is $n^2 - n$.

a Which number appears in both sequences and in the same position?

b Otis says that there are only three terms in the quadratic sequence that are not in the arithmetic sequence. Explain why Otis is correct and write down these three terms.

DF **ES** **4** Here is a pattern made from dots.

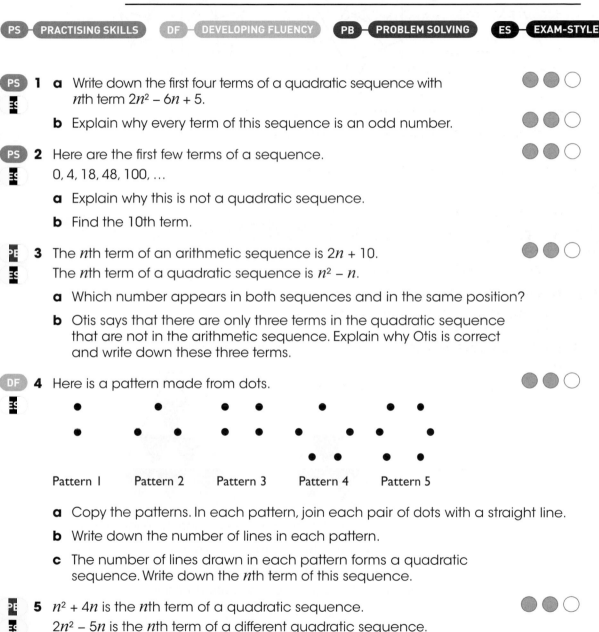

Pattern 1   Pattern 2   Pattern 3   Pattern 4   Pattern 5

a Copy the patterns. In each pattern, join each pair of dots with a straight line.

b Write down the number of lines in each pattern.

c The number of lines drawn in each pattern forms a quadratic sequence. Write down the nth term of this sequence.

PB **ES** **5** $n^2 + 4n$ is the nth term of a quadratic sequence.

$2n^2 - 5n$ is the nth term of a different quadratic sequence.

a Angus says that the number 12 appears in both sequences. Is Angus right? Explain your answer.

b For what value of n is the term the same in both sequences?

MATHEMATICS ONLY

DF **ES** **6** In this pattern, lines are drawn from each vertex to the mid-point of each side inside some regular polygons.

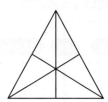
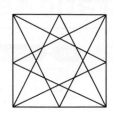
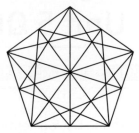

a Write down the number of lines drawn inside each of these polygons.

b How many lines would there be inside a regular hexagon?

c The number of lines in the pattern forms a quadratic sequence. Write down the nth term for this sequence.

d How many lines would there be in a 12-sided regular polygon?

PB **ES** **7** Here are five of the first six terms of a quadratic sequence.

2   4   7   ...   16   22

a Write down the missing term.

b What is the 20th term of this sequence?

c Write down the position-to-term formula.

DF **ES** **8** Here is a pattern made from black and white triangular tiles.

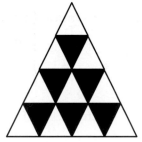

a Write down an expression in terms of n for the sequence of black triangles.

b Write down an expression in terms of n for the sequence of white triangles.

c Show that the sequence formed by the total number of small triangles in each pattern is the sequence of square numbers.

Algebra Strand 2 Sequences Unit 6 nth term of a quadratic sequence

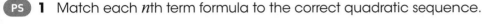

PS – PRACTISING SKILLS   **DF** – DEVELOPING FLUENCY   **PB** – PROBLEM SOLVING   **ES** – EXAM-STYLE

PS **1** Match each nth term formula to the correct quadratic sequence.

    a $n^2 + 3n$ **A** 6, 8, 8, 6, 2

    b $2n^2 - n - 5$ **B** 0, –1.5, –4, –7.5, –12

    c $5n - n^2 + 2$ **C** –4, 1, 10, 23, 40

    d $\dfrac{1 - n^2}{2}$ **D** 4, 10, 18, 28, 40

PB **2** Bilal started a computer company in 2010. The profits of the
ES company, in £ millions, for the first five years from 2010 were
0, 2, 6, 12, 20. If this pattern continues

    a what profit might Bilal expect to make in the next year?

    b what profit might Bilal expect to make after n years of the company's
existence?

    c in what year will the profits first exceed £100 million?

PB **3** The nth term of a sequence is given by $n^2 + n + 1$.
ES

    a Kyle says that all the terms in this sequence are prime numbers.
Show that Kyle is wrong.

    b How many of the first ten terms are not prime numbers?

PB **4** Here are the first three patterns in a sequence of patterns made
ES from triangles and hexagons.

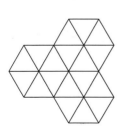
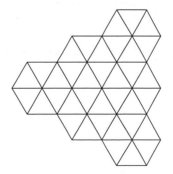

S is the sequence of the number of edges of the hexagons in each pattern. T is the sequence of the number of edges of the small triangles in each pattern.

The sequence formed by subtracting sequence T, term by term, from sequence S has an nth term given by $an^2 + bn$.

Work out the values of a and b.

PB
ES
5 The nth term of a sequence is given by $n^2 - 2n + 5$. The nth term of a different sequence is given by $n^2 + n - 7$.

   a Which term has the same value and is in the same position in both sequences?

   b Explain why this is the only common term.

PS
6 Work out the nth term of each of these quadratic sequences.

   a 2, 2, 0, –4, –10

   b –1, 0, 2, 5, 9

   c –6, –4, 0, 6, 14

   d –6, –4, 6, 24, 50

DF
ES
7 Here are the first three patterns in a sequence of patterns made from sticks.

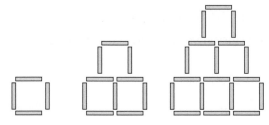

   a Work out the number of sticks in the nth pattern.

   b What is the greatest value of n that can be made with 200 sticks?

PB
ES
8 Here are the first five terms of a quadratic expression.

   5   24   55   98   153

The nth term of this sequence is written in the form $an^2 + bn + c$.

   a Work out the values of a, b and c.

   b Prove that all the even numbered terms are even numbers.

Algebra Strand 3 Functions and graphs Unit 3 The equation of a straight line

MATHEMATICS ONLY

PS – **PRACTISING SKILLS**   **DF** – **DEVELOPING FLUENCY**   **PB** – **PROBLEM SOLVING**   **ES** – **EXAM-STYLE**

PS **1** Here are some lines drawn on a co-ordinate grid.

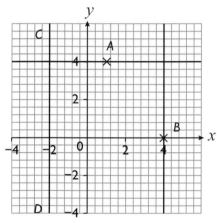

a Write down the equation of

   i the horizontal line passing through A

   ii the vertical line passing through B

   iii the line CD.

b Draw the lines with equation

   i $x = 2.5$

   ii $y = -3$.

PB **2** Here are equations of two lines.
ES

$y = 1.5x - 4$ $3x - 2y = 4$

Brian says the two lines are parallel. Jane says the two lines have the same y-intercept.

a Who is right, Brian or Jane, or are they both right?

b Write down the gradient of $y = 1.5x - 4$.

PB **3** Here are some lines drawn on a co-ordinate grid.

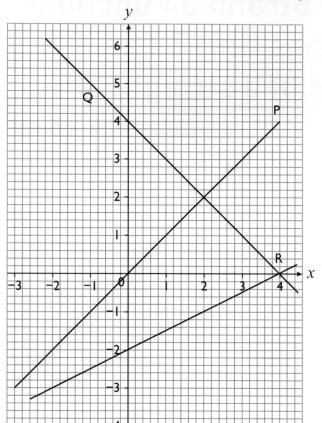

a Write down an equation for

i P

ii Q

iii R.

b On a copy of the grid, draw the lines with equations

i $y = 3x$

ii $x - y = 3$.

PB **4** The diagram shows the line PQ. A line, L, is parallel to PQ and
ES passes through the point (9, 0). Find an equation of the line L.

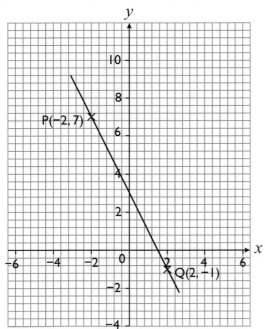

PB **5** A is a point with co-ordinates (5, 3). B is a point with co-ordinates (3, −7).
ES **a** Work out an equation of a straight line passing through A and B.
Another straight line, L, has y intercept of 1. L is parallel to AB.

b Find an equation of L.

PB **6** The line, M, passes through the point (−2, 5). It is parallel to the
ES line with equation $x + y = 5$.

a Find an equation of the line M.
The line with equation $y = 2x$ intersects M at the point B.

b Work out the co-ordinates of the point B.

c Find the value of x when $y = 8$.

Algebra Strand 3 Functions and graphs Unit 4 Plotting quadratic and cubic graphs

PS — **PRACTISING SKILLS**   **DF** — **DEVELOPING FLUENCY**   **PB** — **PROBLEM SOLVING**   **ES** — **EXAM-STYLE**

PS **1** **a** This is a table of values for $y = x^2 + 3x - 5$. Work out the missing values in the table.

x	–3	–2	–1	0	1	2	3	4
y	–5			–5		5		

b This is a table of values for $y = 1 + 2x - 3x^2$. Work out the missing values in the table.

x	–3	–2	–1	0	1	2	3	4
y		–15			0			–39

PS **2** **a** This is a table of values for $y = x^3 - x + 4$. Work out the missing values in the table.

x	–3	–2	–1	0	1	2	3	4
y		–2		4	4			64

b This is a table of values for $y = 2x^3 - 6x^2 + 3x - 1$. Work out the missing values in the table.

x	–3	–2	–1	0	1	2	3	4
y			–12		–2		8	

DF **3** The diagram on p. 55 shows part of the graph of $y = 2x^2 - x - 6$.

   a Write down the co-ordinates of the y-intercept.

   b Write down the solutions of the equation $2x^2 - x - 6 = 0$.

   c By considering the line $y = -3$, estimate the solutions of the equation $2x^2 - x - 3 = 0$.

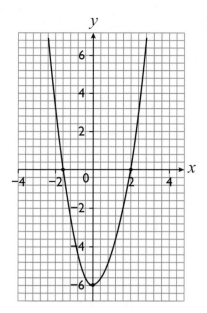

DF **4** The diagram shows part of the graph of $y = x^3 - 2x^2 - 3x$.

    a Write down the solutions of the equation $x^3 - 2x^2 - 3x = 0$.

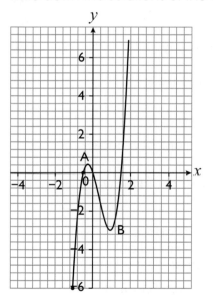

    b Estimate the co-ordinates of the points A and B.

    c Show that the equation $x^3 - 2x^2 - 3x = 4$ has just one solution.

DF **ES** **5** This is a table of values for $y = x^2 - 2x - 3$.

x	–3	–2	–1	0	1	2	3	4
y		5		–3				5

    a Work out the missing values in the table.

    b Draw a graph of $y = x^2 - 2x - 3$.

    c Use your graph to solve $x^2 - 2x - 3 = 0$.

    d Estimate solutions of the equation $x^2 - 2x - 5 = 0$.

DF **ES** **6** This is a table of values for $y = x^3 - 2x^2 - 5x + 6$.

x	–3	–2	–1	0	1	2	3	4
y				6			0	

    a Work out the missing values in the table.

    b Draw a graph of $y = x^3 - 2x^2 - 5x + 6$.

    c Use your graph to solve $x^3 - 2x^2 - 5x + 6 = 0$.

DF **ES** **7** **a** Draw a graph of $y = 3 + x - 4x^2$.

    b Use your graph to solve $3 + x - 4x^2 = 0$.

    c Estimate solutions of the equation $3 + x - 4x^2 = 0$.

DF **ES** **8** On the same axes, draw graphs of $y = x^3 - x$ and $y = x$.
The graphs cross at points A, B and C.

    a Write down the co-ordinates of points A, B and C.

    b The x-co-ordinates of A, B and C are the solutions of a cubic equation. Write down this equation.

    c Write down the equation of a straight line you could draw to solve $x^3 - 3x = 3$.

PB **ES** **9** A cricket ball is thrown vertically up from 2 metres above the ground. Its path is modelled by the quadratic function $h = 2 + 9t - 5t^2$ where h is the height of the ball and t the time.

    a Draw the graph of h against t for values of t from 0 to 2 at intervals of 0.25.

    b Use your graph to find the greatest height the ball reaches from the ground.

Algebra Strand 3 Functions and graphs Unit 5 Finding equations of straight lines

PS — PRACTISING SKILLS   DF — DEVELOPING FLUENCY   PB — PROBLEM SOLVING   ES — EXAM-STYLE

PS **1** Write down the equation of the line that has a gradient of

   a 6 and goes through $(1, 5)$

   b -4 and goes through $(3, 10)$

   c 3.5 and goes through $(-2, -12)$.

DF **2** Triangle PQR is drawn on a co-ordinate grid.

   a Write down the equations of the three lines that make this triangle.

   b Work out the area of triangle PQR.

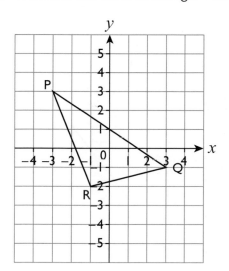

PB
ES

3 The graph shows the prices charged by Safe Car Hire.

It shows the relationship between the charge (£C) and the number of days (n) for which the car is hired.

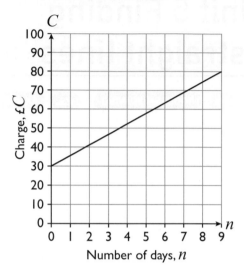

Number of days, n

a i Write down the gradient of this graph.

ii What does this gradient represent?

b Write down the equation of this straight-line graph.

c Alan hires a car from Safe Car Hire for 20 days. Work out the total charge.

PB
ES

4 The graph shows the time, T minutes, to cook a turkey with mass m lb.

T is given by the formula $T = am + b$.

a Work out the values of a and b.

b Work out the cooking time of a turkey with a mass of 26 lb.

Give your answer in hours and minutes.

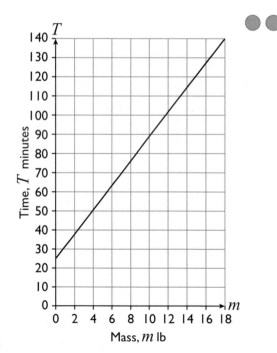

Mass, m lb

5 Line l goes through the points A(0, 5) and B(5, 0).
Line m goes through the points D(0, 2) and C(2, 0).

  a Write down the equation of each line.

  b Work out the area of the quadrilateral ABCD.

6 The two straight lines, p and q, are drawn on a co-ordinate grid.

  a Write down the equation of each line.

  b Write down the equation of the straight line that is parallel to p and passes through (1, 5).

  c What are the co-ordinates of the point where lines p and q intersect?

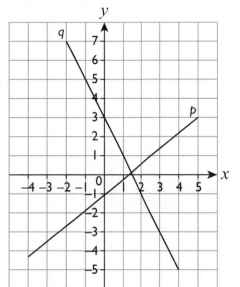

7 A square has vertices A(3, 3), B(3, −2), C(−2, −2) and D(−2, 3).

  a Write down the equations of the diagonals.

  b What is the product of the gradients of the two diagonals?

8 a Write down the gradient of the straight line that joins the points E(5, 8) and F(−3, 20).

  b Toby says that the straight line that goes through E and F will extend through the point G(40, −45).
  Is Toby right?

9 Line l passes through points A(7, 2) and B(4, 4).
Line m has equation $2x + 3y = 5$.

  a Prove that l and m are parallel.

  b Line n has gradient 1.5 and passes through the mid-point of AB.
  Write down the equation for n.

10 A quadrilateral has vertices A(4, 5), B(9, 2), C(1, −1) and D(−4, 2).

  a Prove that ABCD is a parallelogram.

  b Write down the equation of the line that passes through A and C.

Algebra Strand 3 Functions and graphs Unit 6 Perpendicular lines

PS **PRACTISING SKILLS**   **DF** **DEVELOPING FLUENCY**   **PB** **PROBLEM SOLVING**   **ES** **EXAM-STYLE**

PS **1** Look at the diagram.

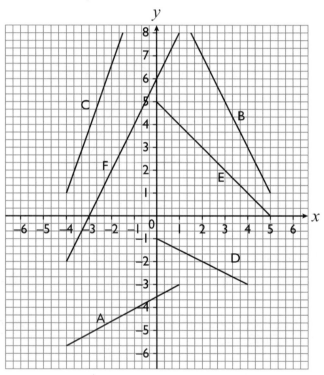

a Which of the lines on the grid are

  i parallel
  ii perpendicular

  to the line with equation $y = 2x - 3$?

b Write down an equation of each of the lines chosen in part **a**.

PS
ES
2 Write down the gradient of a line perpendicular to the line with equation:

a $y = 2x - 1$

b $y = 1 - 2x$

c $2y = 1 - x$

d $x + 3y = 1$

e $y - 1 = \dfrac{2x}{3}$

f $5x + 4y = 20$

DF
ES
3 ABC is a right-angled triangle. Angle A = 90°.

a Write down an equation of the line AB.

b Find the co-ordinates of B.

c Work out the area of triangle ABC.

PS
ES
4 Here are the equations of eight straight lines.

A $y = 2x - 3$ **B** $y = 5 - 3x$ **C** $3y - x = 7$ **D** $x + y = 3$

E $y = \dfrac{2x - 1}{2}$ **F** $y = 3(1 - x)$ **G** $y = \dfrac{x}{3} - 2$ **H** $x = 3(y + 2)$

a Which lines are parallel?

b Which lines are perpendicular to each other?

PB
ES
5 Find an equation of a line perpendicular to $y = 4x + 3$ passing through the point (1, 7).

6 a Draw the line with equation $2y = x - 2$. Use the same scale on each axis.

b Find an equation of the line perpendicular to $2y = x - 2$ passing through $(2, 0)$.

c Work out the area of the triangle bounded by this perpendicular, the line $2y = x - 2$ and the y-axis.

7 a L is a line with equation $2x + 3y = 6$. On a grid, draw L.

b The point $(6, -2)$ lies on L. P is a straight line perpendicular to L passing through $(6, -2)$. Find an equation for P.

c Find the co-ordinates of the intercepts of P with the axes.

d Find the area bounded by L, P and the x-axis.

8 AC is a diagonal of a kite ABCD.

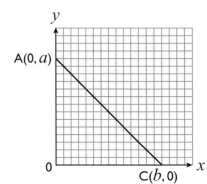

Prove that the equation of the other diagonal can be written as
$$y = \frac{2bx + a^2 - b^2}{2a}.$$

9 $A(2, 2)$ and $B(12, 2)$ are the end points of a diameter of a semicircle. The point $P(4, 6)$ is a point on the circumference of the semicircle.

Find the equation of the tangent to the semicircle at P.

10 ABCD is a square. $A(4, 6)$ lies on the line with equation $y = 0.5x + 4$. The perpendicular to $y = 0.5x + 4$ passing through A meets the x-axis at B. AB is one side of the square ABCD.

Find the co-ordinates of the points C and D.

Algebra Strand 3 Functions and graphs Unit 7 Polynomial and reciprocal functions

PS — **PRACTISING SKILLS**   **DF** — **DEVELOPING FLUENCY**   **PB** — **PROBLEM SOLVING**   **ES** — **EXAM-STYLE**

PS
ES

1 A curve has the equation $y = x^3 - 2x^2 - 4x$.

  a Copy and complete the table of values for the function.

x	-2	-1	0	1	2	3	4
y	-8		0			-3	

  b Draw the graph of $y = x^3 - 2x^2 - 4x$.

  c Use your graph to estimate solutions of the equation
     $x^3 - 2x^2 - 4x + 5 = 0$.

PB
ES

2 The volume V of this cuboid is given by the formula $V = x(x - 2)(x - 4)$.

  a Draw a graph of V against x taking values of x from 0 to 5.

  b Use your graph to estimate the dimensions of the cuboid when $V = 2$.
     Explain why only one value of x is acceptable.

PS
ES

3 a Copy and complete this table for $y = x + \dfrac{1}{x}$.

x	-8	-4	-2	-0.5	-0.25	0	0.25	0.5	2	4	8
y	-8.125				-4.25				2.5		

  b Sketch a graph of $y = x + \dfrac{1}{x}$.

DF **4** The graph shows the curve $y = x^3 - 4x$.

ES

a Write down all the roots of the equation $x^3 - 4x = 0$.

b Write down the co-ordinates of all turning points.

c Use this graph to estimate the solutions of

   i $x^3 - 4x - 2 = 0$

   ii $x^3 - 2x = 0$.

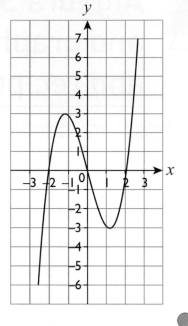

DF **5** Sketch graphs of the following equations.

For each sketch, write down the co-ordinates of any turning points and any x- or y-intercepts.

a $y = x - x^3$

b $y = 1 - \dfrac{1}{x}$

c $y = x^3 + 1$

PB **6 a** Copy and complete the table of values for $y = x^2 + x - \dfrac{1}{x}$.

ES

x	-3	-2	-1	-0.5	-0.25	0	0.25	0.5	1	2	3
y	6.33		1		3.8125		-3.6875		1	5.5	

b Draw the graph of $y = x^2 + x - \dfrac{1}{x}$.

c Use your graph to estimate

   i the co-ordinates of the turning point

   ii the solution of $x^2 + x - \dfrac{1}{x} = 0$.

PB **7 a** On the same pair of axes, draw the graphs of $y = x^2 - x$ and

ES $y = 2 - \dfrac{1}{x}$.

b Show that the points of intersection of these two graphs are solutions of the equation $x^3 - x^2 - 2x + 1 = 0$.

c What is the approximate positive value of each solution?

Algebra Strand 3 Functions and graphs Unit 8 Exponential functions

PS — PRACTISING SKILLS   **DF** — DEVELOPING FLUENCY   **PB** — PROBLEM SOLVING   **ES** — EXAM-STYLE

PS **ES** **1** This is a table of values for $y = 1.5^x$.

x	–2	–1	0	1	2	3	4
y	0.44		1		2.25		

a Work out the missing values in this table of values.

b Draw a grid with x values from –2 to 4 and y values from –1 to 8. Draw the graph of $y = 1.5^x$.

c Use your graph to estimate the value of x for which $1.5^x = 3$.

PS **ES** **2** This is a table of values for $y = 100 \times 4^{-x}$.

x	–2	–1	0	1	2	3	4
y	1600			25		1.5625	

a Work out the missing values in this table of values.

b Draw a sketch of the graph of $y = 100 \times 4^{-x}$ showing the value of the y-intercept, which is at the point P.

PS **ES** **3** A curve has equation $y = a^x$ where a is a positive constant.

a Write down the coordinates of the point where this curve crosses the y-axis.

b The curve passes through the point with coordinates (3, 15.625). Work out the value of a.

c Work out the value of y when
  i $x = 0$
  ii $x = 2$.

PB **ES** **4** Riaz invests £2000 into a bank account paying compound interest at a rate of 3% per year. Irfan invests £2500 into a different bank account paying compound interest at a rate of 1.5% per year.

The amount of money, £y, in a bank account after x years is given by the formula $y = P \times a^x$ where £P is the amount of money invested and a is a multiplication factor.

a Show that for Riaz's investment, $y = 2000 \times 1.03^x$.

b Find the formula for Irfan's investment.

c By drawing graphs of each formula, find an estimate for the value of x for which the values of both investments are the same. Give your answer to the nearest whole number.

DF **ES** **5** The points $(1, 10)$ and $(4, 80)$ lie on the curve with equation $y = ab^x$, where a and b are integers. If the points $(3, q)$ and $(p, 200)$ lie on the curve, find the values of q and p.

PB **ES** **6** A rubber ball is dropped from a height of x metres. Each time the ball strikes the floor it rebounds to $\frac{4}{5}$ of the height it has just fallen.

a If the ball is dropped from a height of 15 metres, what distance will it have travelled when it hits the floor for the 4th time?

b Write down an expression, in terms of x and n, for the height of the ball after n bounces.

c Brian says the ball will carry on bouncing forever. Explain why Brian is wrong.

DF **ES** **7** The diagram shows a sketch of a curve with equation $y = pq^x$ where p and q are constants.

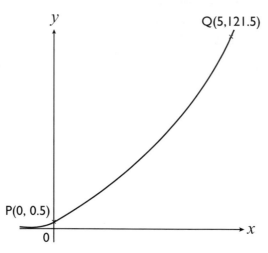

a Find the values of p and q.

b Find the value of r if $(-4, r)$ is a point on this curve.

PB
ES
8 A population of a certain species of bird is decreasing by 25% every year. At the start of 2010, the population of this species of bird was estimated at 2 million.

   a What was the population at the end of 2015?

   b If P is the population after x years, write down a formula for P in terms of x.

   c Estimate the year in which this species of bird is likely to become extinct.

PB
ES
9 Elfyn borrows £15000 to buy a car. Each year, Elfyn repays 15% of the money that he still owes.

   a How much does Elfyn owe after

     i 4 years?

     ii n years?

   b As soon as Elfyn owes no more than £500, he pays off the remaining amount. How many years will it take Elfyn to repay what he owes?

PB
ES
10 In 1985, Sioned bought a painting for £4500. The value of the painting increased by 20% each year. In 1990, Ellis bought a painting for £15000. The value of Ellis's painting increased by 12% each year.

   £V is the value of a painting after n years.

   a Write down an equation for V, in terms of n, for each of these two paintings.

   b In what year was Sioned's painting first worth more than Ellis's painting?

   c In what year did the value of Sioned's painting exceed £1 million?

Algebra Strand 3 Functions and graphs Unit 9 Trigonometric functions

PS — **PRACTISING SKILLS**   **DF** — **DEVELOPING FLUENCY**   **PB** — **PROBLEM SOLVING**   **ES** — **EXAM-STYLE**

DF **1** This is a table of values for $y = \sin x$.

x	0°	15°	30°	45°	60°	75°	90°
y	0		0.5				1.0

a Work out the missing values in this table of values.

b On a suitable grid, draw the graph of $y = \sin x$ for values of x from 0° to 90°.

c Use this table to find
  i $\sin 120°$
  ii $\sin 135°$
  iii $\sin 210°$
  iv $\sin 330°$
  v $\sin 195°$
  vi $\sin 105°$
  vii $\sin 315°$
  viii $\sin 285°$

PS **2** $\sin x = 0.5$
Which of the following are also equal to 0.5?
  a $\sin 150°$ **b** $\cos 30°$ **c** $\cos 150°$ **d** $\cos 60°$ **e** $\sin 210°$
  f $\tan 150°$ **g** $\sin 390°$ **h** $\cos 300°$ **i** $\tan 30°$ **j** $\sin 330°$

DF
ES

3 The diagram shows the graphs of two trigonometric functions,
$y = \sin x$ and $y = \cos x$.

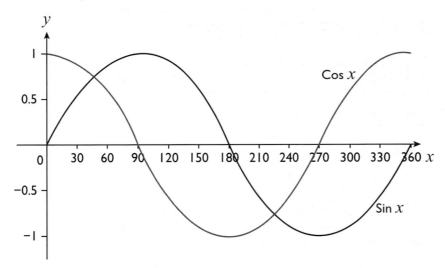

a Which is the graph of each function?

b For what values of x between 0° and 360° does $\sin x = \cos x$?

c Work out the difference between $\sin x$ and $\cos x$ when $x = 150°$.

DF **4** Write down

a the minimum value of y and

b the maximum value of y when

   i $y = \sin x$

   ii $y = \tan x$

   iii $y = \cos x$

   iv $y = \sin 2x$

   v $y = 2\sin x$

   vi $y = 5\sin 100x$

   vii $y = \dfrac{1}{2}\cos 2x$

   viii $y = 1 + \cos 4x$

   ix $y = \sin 5x + 3$

   x $y = 3 - 2\sin x$

PB
ES
5 The London Eye is a tourist attraction where visitors sit in passenger cars on the outer edge of a giant revolving wheel.

The highest point on the London Eye is about 130 metres above the ground. The centre is about 70 metres above the ground.

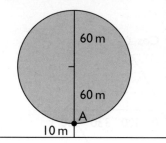

60 m

60 m

A

10 m

The London Eye starts to rotate at a time $t = 0$ minutes when A is at its lowest point. The distance, y metres, of A above the ground after t minutes is given by the equation $y = a + b \sin wt$ where a, b and w are integers.

If it takes 30 minutes for the point A to reach its highest point, find the values of a, b and w.

PB
ES
6 The distance, y metres, of a particle from a given point O after t seconds is given by the formula $y = 6 + 4 \cos 10t$.

a Draw a graph of $y = 6 + 4 \cos 10t$ from $t = 0$ to $t = 18$ in steps of three seconds.

b For how many seconds is the particle more than five metres away from O?

c Find an estimate for the distance of the particle from O after five seconds.

7 Here are sketches of the graphs of five functions.

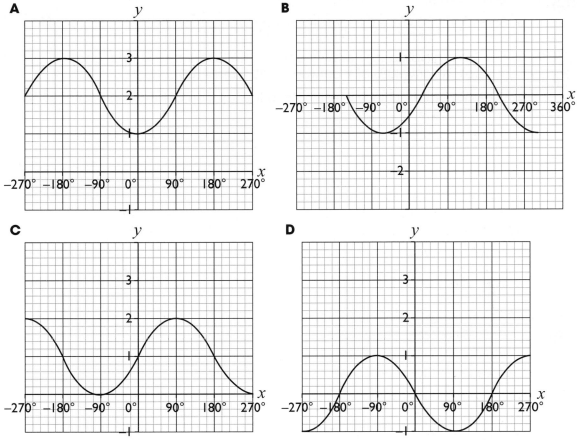

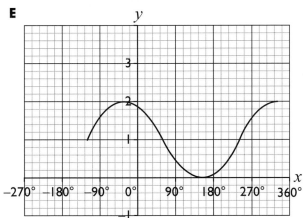

Match each of these functions with one of the graphs A to E.

i $y = \sin x + 1$ **ii** $y = -\sin x$ **iii** $y = 2 - \cos x$ **iv** $y = \sin(x - 30)$ **v** $y = \cos(x + 30) + 1$

DF
ES
8 a Write down all the values of x between 0° and 360° for which $\cos x = -0.5$.

b Solve $1 + 2 \cos 5x = 0$ for values of x between 0° and 90°.

PB
ES
9 a On 2 mm graph paper, draw graphs of the functions $y = \tan x$ and $y = \cos 2x$ for values of x between –180° and +180°.

b Use your graph to find an estimate to the solution of $\tan x = \cos 2x$ when $0° < x < 90°$.

Algebra Strand 4 Algebraic methods Unit 1 Trial and improvement

PS — PRACTISING SKILLS   **DF** — DEVELOPING FLUENCY   **PB** — PROBLEM SOLVING   **ES** — EXAM-STYLE

DF **1** The equation $x^3 + 2x = 25$ has a solution between 2 and 3.

    a Calculate this solution correct to 1 decimal place.

    b What test must always be carried out to confirm that the solution is accurate to 1 decimal place?

DF **2** A solution to the equation $2b^3 - b - 42.5 = 0$ lies between 2 and 3.
Find this solution correct to 2 decimal places.

DF **3** The equation $4x^3 - 50x = 917.7$ has a solution between 6 and 7.

    a Calculate this solution correct to 1 decimal place.

    b What test must always be carried out to confirm that the solution is accurate to 1 decimal place?

PB **4** The product of $e^2 + 1$ and $e - 1$ is 420.5
Use a trial and improvement method to find a positive value of e correct to 1 decimal place.

PB **5** The equation $x(x - 1)(x + 5) = 384$ has a solution between 6 and 7.

    a Find this solution correct to 2 decimal places.

    b How did your confirm your solution to know that it was accurate to 2 decimal places?

PB **6** The base of a box is a square.
The height of the box is twice the length of one of the lengths of the base of the box.
The volume of the box is 194.67 cm.
Use a trial and improvement method to find the dimensions of the box, with each measurement correct to 1 decimal place.

PB **7** A triangle has a base of length $(x + 2)$ cm and a perpendicular height of $(x - 5)$ cm.
The area of the triangle is 33.5 cm².
Use a trial and improvement method to find the perpendicular height of the triangle correct to 1 decimal place.

Algebra Strand 4 Algebraic methods Unit 2 Linear inequalities

PS PRACTISING SKILLS   **DF** DEVELOPING FLUENCY   **PB** PROBLEM SOLVING   **ES** EXAM-STYLE

PS **1** Solve these inequalities.

    a $4 - 2x \geqslant 8$

    b $3 + 2x < 5x - 9$

    c $2(x + 3) + 3(2x + 5) \geqslant 37$

PS **ES** **2** **a** Write down the inequality shown on this number line.

```
      ○─────────────────────●
  ─5  ─4  ─3  ─2  ─1   0   1   2   3   4   5   x
```

    b Show the inequality $-1 \leqslant x < 5$ on a number line.

    c Solve $2x + 3 > 8$.

DF **3** Colin earns £N each year.

Brian earns at least twice as much as Colin.

Becky earns less than half of what Colin earns.

If Brian earns £x each year and Becky earns £y each year, write inequalities to show their earnings in terms of N.

PB **ES** **4** Paris thinks of a number greater than 5.

She subtracts 3 from the number, then doubles the result.

Her final answer is less than 12.

Write down all the possible numbers Paris could have thought of.

PB **ES** **5** The perimeter of this rectangle is at least 44 cm, but less than 50 cm.

Write down an inequality to show the possible values of x.

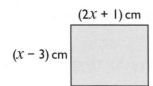

$(2x + 1)$ cm

$(x - 3)$ cm

6 April, Bavinda and Chas each have some marbles.

April has 15 more marbles than Bavinda.

Bavinda has three times as many marbles as Chas.

Together they have less than 200 marbles.

What is the greatest number of marbles that April can have?

7 Write down an inequality for each of the four boundaries of the shaded region.

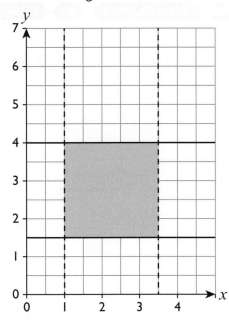

8 On graph paper, show the region that satisfies the inequalities $2 \leqslant x < 4$ and $2.5 \leqslant y < 4.5$.

9 The length, width and height of this cuboid satisfy the following inequalities:

$10 \leqslant l < 11 \quad 3 \leqslant w < 3.5 \quad 6 \leqslant h < 8$

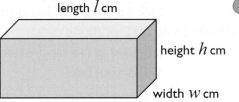

length l cm

height h cm

width w cm

  a Work out the greatest possible volume of the cuboid.

  b Work out the smallest possible surface area of the cuboid.

10 n is an integer that satisfies the inequality $5n - 1 > 4n + 2$.

Which one of these inequalities can n not satisfy?

$4n + 5 > n + 2 \qquad 2n - 7 > 1 - n \qquad n + 4 > 6n - 8 \qquad 7 - n > 2n - 11$

11 n is an integer that satisfies both of these inequalities:

$4n - 1 < 2n + 3$ and $5(n + 4) \geqslant 2(n + 5)$

Write down all the possible values of n.

Algebra Strand 4 Algebraic methods Unit 3 Solving pairs of equations by substitution

PS — PRACTISING SKILLS   DF — DEVELOPING FLUENCY   PB — PROBLEM SOLVING   ES — EXAM-STYLE

PS 1 Solve these pairs of simultaneous equations by substitution.

   a $2x + y = 6$
      $y = x + 3$

   b $x + 4y = 11$
      $x = y + 1$

   c $2x + 3y = 6$
      $x = 5 - 2y$

DF 2 Aled thinks of two numbers.
The difference between the two numbers is 7.
The sum of the two numbers is 25.
What two numbers is Aled thinking of?

DF 3 The sum of two numbers is 160.
The difference between the two numbers is 102.
Work out the two numbers.

PB 4 Elfyn pays £10.50 for 4 portions of fish and 3 portions of chips
Tracey pays £5.40 for 3 portions of fish.
Malcolm buys 2 portions of fish and 2 portions of chips.
How much should this cost him?

PB 5 Chan has exactly 24 notes in his wallet.
They are either £20 notes or £10 notes.
The total value of the notes is £410.
How many £20 notes are in Chan's wallet?

PB 6 What is the perimeter of this rectangle?

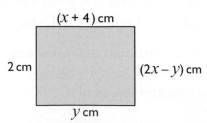

$(x + 4)$ cm

2 cm

$(2x - y)$ cm

y cm

7 In Year 10:

- There are b boys and g girls.

- There are 45 more boys than girls.

If 12 boys and no girls joined Year 10, there would be twice as many boys as there are girls.

How many students are in Year 10?

8 A train carriage has t tables that have seats for 4 people and s single seats (with no tables).

The total number of seats in a carriage is 62 and there are 22 more single seats than tables.

In one carriage, 19 of the single seats are occupied.

How many of the single seats are not occupied?

9 A tennis club has f female members and m male members.

In 2010, they had 16 more female members than male members.

By 2015, the number of female members had increased by one-third, the number of male members had decreased by 18 and there were a total of 120 members.

How many female members did the club have in 2010?

10 An equation of line l is given by $y = mx + c$.

The points $(1, 7)$ and $(3, 11)$ lie on line l.

Work out the values of m and c.

Algebra Strand 4 Algebraic methods Unit 4 Solving simultaneous equations by elimination

PS — PRACTISING SKILLS   DF — DEVELOPING FLUENCY   PB — PROBLEM SOLVING   ES — EXAM-STYLE

DF 1 Solve these pairs of simultaneous equations by elimination.

    a $3x + 2y = 14$
       $5x - 2y = 18$

    b $2x + 3y = 2$
       $8x + 3y = 17$

    c $6x - 5y = 23$
       $4x - 3y = 14$

PB **ES 2** The price of tickets for a football match are £a for adults and £c
for children.

Morgan pays £270 for tickets for 2 adults and 5 children.

Jim pays £251 for tickets for 3 adults and 2 children.

Peter has £150 to buy tickets for the football match. Does he have enough money to buy tickets for himself and his 3 children?

PB **ES 3** A taxi company charges a fixed amount plus an additional cost
per mile.

A journey of 8 miles costs £8.90. A journey of 12 miles costs £12.10.

Sioned is 20 miles from home. She has only £20.

Does Sioned have enough money to travel home by taxi?

DF **ES 4** Work out the area of this rectangle.

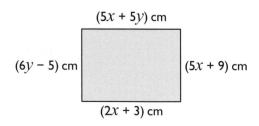

(5x + 5y) cm

(6y − 5) cm   (5x + 9) cm

(2x + 3) cm

5 The Smith family and the Jones family have booked the same summer holiday.

Mr and Mrs Smith and their three children paid £2440.

Mr Jones, his mother and father and his son paid £2330.

After they book, the travel company reduces the cost of a child's holiday by 10% and refunds both families.

How much refund should each family receive?

6 The diagram shows an equilateral triangle and a square.

The perimeter of the square is equal to the perimeter of the triangle.

Work out the area of the square.

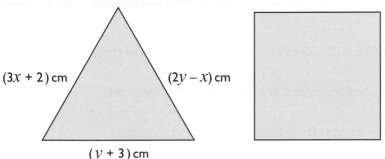

$(3x + 2)$ cm $(2y - x)$ cm

$(y + 3)$ cm

7 A boy travels for x hours at a speed of 5 km/h.

He then travels for y hours at a speed of 10 km/h.

In total, he travels 35 km at an average speed of 7 km/h.

Work out the values of x and y.

8 In one week, Liz works 35 hours at her standard rate of pay and 12 hours at her overtime rate. For this, she is paid £428.40.

In a different week, Liz works 40 hours at her standard rate of pay and 8 hours at her overtime rate. For this, she is paid £425.60.

a Work out Liz's standard rate of pay.

b Work out the ratio of the standard rate of pay to the overtime rate of pay.

9 Two people bought identical Christmas decorations from the same shop.

One paid £65.60 for 200 streamers and 220 tree decorations.

The other paid £63.30 for 210 streamers and 200 tree decorations.

How much would it cost to buy 200 streamers and 200 tree decorations from this shop?

10 The points $(2, 2.5)$ and $(6, -2.5)$ lie on the line with equation $ax + by = c$.

a Bob says the point $(-2, 8)$ also lies on this line.

Is Bob correct?

b Write down

i the gradient of this line

ii the co-ordinates of the intercepts on the axes.

Algebra Strand 4 Algebraic methods Unit 5 Using graphs to solve simultaneous equations

PS ▸ PRACTISING SKILLS   **DF** ▸ DEVELOPING FLUENCY   **PB** ▸ PROBLEM SOLVING   **ES** ▸ EXAM-STYLE

DF **1** **a** Draw the graphs of $y = 2x + 3$ and $y = 3 - x$ on the same pair of axes.

b Write down the co-ordinates of the point where the two lines intersect.

c Check your answer to part **b** by solving the two equations using algebra.

DF **2** **a** Draw the graphs of $2x + y = 3$ and $x - 2y = 4$ on the same pair of axes.

b Write down the co-ordinates of the point where the two lines intersect.

c Use algebra to check your answer to part **b**.

d Work out the area of the region bounded by the lines $2x + y = 3$ and $x - 2y = 4$ and the y-axis.

PB **3** Taxi companies charge a fixed amount plus an additional cost
ES per mile.

Toni's taxis	Colin's cabs
£2.50 plus £1.20 per mile.	£5.00 plus 75p per mile.

a On the same pair of axes, draw graphs to show the cost, £C, of a journey of x miles for each taxi company.

b What useful information does the point of intersection of the two graphs give you?

c Harry wants to travel 7 miles by taxi. Which company would you recommend?

DF **4** By drawing graphs, find the approximate solutions of
ES $$15x + 8y = 60$$
$$4x - 9y = 54$$

MATHEMATICS ONLY

PS **5** Line l has equation $x + y = 5$.
Line m has equation $y = 3x + 3$.
Line n has equation $y = x + 1$.
By looking at the graph, solve each pair of simultaneous equations.

a $x + y = 5$
$y = x + 1$

b $y = 3x + 3$
$y = x + 1$

c $x + y = 5$
$y = 3x + 3$

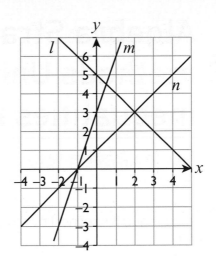

PB **ES** **6** Two cars are travelling towards each other along a straight road.
The distance, d metres, from O after t seconds is given for each car by

Car A $d = 10 + 30t$ **Car B** $d = 120 - 20t$

a On the same axes, draw graphs to show this information.

b Use your graphs to help answer these questions.

i At what time were both cars the same distance from O?

ii How far from O were the cars at this time?

PB **ES** **7** The graph shows the speed, v metres per second, of a car after t seconds.

a Write down the equation of this graph in the form $v = u + at$, where u and a are constants.

b The speed of a second car is given by the equation $v = 80 - 2.5t$. Draw this line on a copy of the graph.

c **i** After how many seconds are the two cars travelling at the same speed?

ii Estimate this speed.

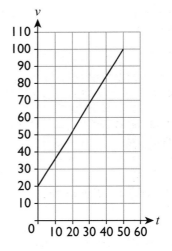

PS **8** **a** Write down the equation of the straight line that passes through

i A and C **ii** D and B.

b Write down the co-ordinates of the point of intersection of the two equations in part **a**.

c Use algebra to check your answer to part **b**.

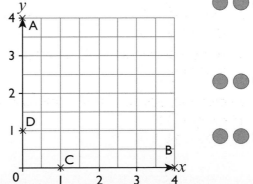

Algebra Strand 4 Algebraic methods Unit 6 Solving linear inequalities in two variables

PS — PRACTISING SKILLS   **DF** — DEVELOPING FLUENCY   **PB** — PROBLEM SOLVING   **ES** — EXAM-STYLE

PS **1** Write down the inequality defined by the shaded region in each of these diagrams.

a

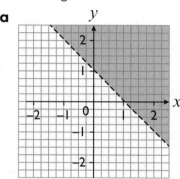

b

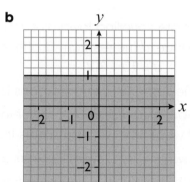

c

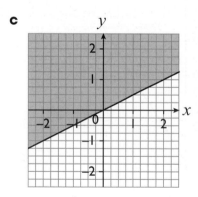

d

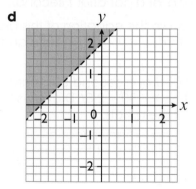

DF
ES **2** Draw a diagram to show the region defined by the inequalities

$x + y \leqslant 4$ $y < 3$ $x \geqslant -1$ $y > x$

DF **3** **a** Write down the three inequalities which define this shaded region.

b Find the maximum value of $x + y$ in this region.

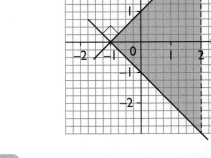

DF **4** A region A is defined by the inequalities $x + y \geqslant 3, x \leqslant 3$ and $y \leqslant x + 1$.

a Show this region on a diagram.

b The points (a, b) are points inside A, where a and b are integers. Write down the co-ordinates of each of these points.

5 Find the area, in square units, o.f the region defined by the inequalities $2x + 3y \leqslant 6, y > x + 1$ and $x \geqslant -1$.

6 Andy plays in a tennis tournament. The maximum number of matches he can play is 16. Andy wins (W) at least three times as many matches as he loses (L). He wins more than seven matches.

a Write down as many inequalities as you can in W and L.

b Show your inequalities on a diagram.

c If Andy gets 2 points for a win and 1 point for a loss, work out the least number of points that he could get if he plays in just 10 matches.

7 Jamil has a drawer containing 15 pairs of socks. He has more black socks than white socks. The difference between the number of black socks and the number of white socks is less than 12.

a Draw a diagram to show this information.

b Jamil's mum says that he has four pairs of white socks and nine pairs of black socks in his drawer. Is she right?

PB **8**
ES

Farmer Ted has some pigs and some chickens on his farm. The shaded region on the diagram shows the possible numbers of pigs, p, and chickens, c.

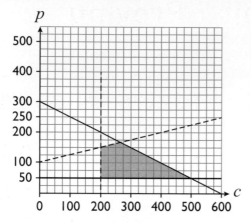

a Describe fully, in words, the relationships between the number of pigs and the number of chickens on Ted's farm.

b The shaded region on the diagram shows the possible numbers of pigs and chickens. Work out the greatest possible total number of pigs and chickens on Ted's farm.

PB **9**
ES

Pete is a property developer. He buys t terraced houses and a apartments. Pete buys no more than eight properties. He wants to have at least two more apartments than terraced houses.

a Write down four inequalities relating to t and a.

b Show these inequalities on a diagram.

c Each terraced house costs £120 000 and each apartment costs £150 000. Work out the greatest amount of money that Pete will have to spend.

Algebra Strand 4 Algebraic methods Unit 7 Proving identities

PS — **PRACTISING SKILLS**   **DF** — **DEVELOPING FLUENCY**   **PB** — **PROBLEM SOLVING**   **ES** — **EXAM-STYLE**

PS ES **1** **a** Show that the difference between two prime numbers is sometimes a prime number and sometimes not.

    b Find two prime numbers such that the sum of their squares is **not** an even number.

PB ES **2** Here is a triangle ABC. All angles are measured in degrees.

A

$2x + 30$

B $5x - 20$ $4x + 5$ C

Prove that triangle ABC can never be an isosceles triangle.

PS ES **3** **a** Prove that the product of three consecutive whole numbers is always an even number.

    b Prove that the sum of three consecutive odd numbers is always an odd number.

PS ES **4** **a** Prove that the product of two odd numbers is always an odd number.

    b Prove that the difference between the squares of two consecutive odd numbers is always an even number.

    c What can you say about the sum of the squares of two consecutive odd numbers?

DF ES **5** n is a positive integer. When is each of the following expressions an even number: sometimes, always or never?

    i $2n - 1$ **ii** $n^2 - 1$ **iii** $(4n - 3)^2$ **iv** $n(n + 1)(n - 10)$ **v** $(2n + 7)(3n - 1)$

PB ES **6** $f(n) = n^2 - 4n - 21$

John says that if $n \neq 0$, $f(n)$ is always an even number. Janet says that $f(n)$ is only an even number when n is an odd number. Who is right?

DF **ES** **7** n and a are integers. Prove that $(n - a)^2 - (n + a)^2$ is always an even number divisible by 4.

PB **ES** **8** Here is a triangle.

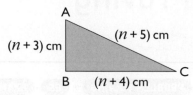

If $n \neq 0$, prove that triangle ABC is **not** a right-angled triangle.

PS **ES** **9** **a** Show that $(x - 4)^2 - (x + 1)^2 = 5(3 - 2x)$.

b Show that $\dfrac{t^2 - 4}{t^2 + t - 2} = \dfrac{t - 2}{t - 1}$

c Show that $(n + 5)(n - 2)(n - 3) = n^3 - 19n + 30$.

Algebra Strand 5 Working with quadratics Unit 1 Factorising quadratics

PS — PRACTISING SKILLS   **DF** — DEVELOPING FLUENCY   **PB** — PROBLEM SOLVING   **ES** — EXAM-STYLE

PS **1** Factorise each expression.

  a $x^2 + 2x$

  b $x^2 - 81$

  c $x^2 - 8x + 4x - 32$

  d $x^2 - 9x + 14$

  e $x^2 + 3x - 40$

  f $x^2 - 9$

PB **2** Amir and Winona factorised $x^2 + 5x - 6$.
ES Amir wrote $x^2 + 5x - 6 = (x + 2)(x + 3)$.
Winona wrote $x^2 + 5x - 6 = (x + 2)(x - 3)$.
Explain why each answer is wrong and give the correct answer.

PB **3** The area of a square is given by the expression $x^2 - 6x + 9$.
ES Write an expression for the side length of the square.

PB **4** The diagram shows three rectangles.
ES

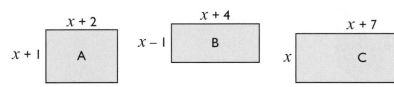

The area of a fourth rectangle D can be found using the equation:
Area D = Area A – Area B + Area C.
What are the dimensions of rectangle D?

DF **5** Work out each of these. Do not use a calculator.

  a $101^2 - 99^2$

  b $63^2 + 2 \times 63 \times 37 + 37^2$

  c $9^4 - 1^4$

6 Bethan thinks of any number, n.

She squares her number, subtracts two times her original number from the result and then subtracts 48.

Write down and fully simplify an expression in n for her final result.

7 The volume of the cuboid shown is $a^3 - 11a^2 + 30a$.

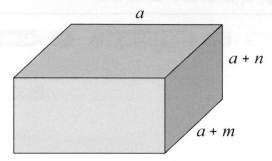

Work out the values of m and n, if $m > n$.

8 Without using a calculator, work out the area of the shaded part of this shape.

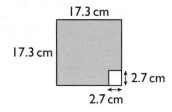

9 In this cuboid:

the area of the front face is given by $p^2 + 17p + 70$

the area of the top face is given by $p^2 + 11p + 28$.

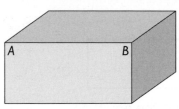

Write down an expression, in terms of p, for the length of the edge AB.

10 Fully factorise this expression.

$$\frac{x^2 + 5x - 24}{x^2 - 9x - 18}$$

Algebra Strand 5 Working with quadratics Unit 2 Solving equations by factorising

PS PRACTISING SKILLS   **DF** DEVELOPING FLUENCY   **PB** PROBLEM SOLVING   **ES** EXAM-STYLE

PS **1** Solve these equations.

     a $(x + 1)(x + 2) = 0$

     b $(x - 4)(x - 5) = 0$

     c $x^2 + 9x = 0$

     d $x^2 - 2x - 24 = 0$

     e $x^2 = 36 - 5x$

PS **2** **a** The solutions of a quadratic equation are $x = 5$ and $x = -3$.
Write down the quadratic equation.

     b The solutions of a quadratic equation are $y = -12$ and $y = -7$.
Write down the quadratic equation.

PB
ES **3** Here is Mnambi's attempt at solving $x^2 - x - 20 = 0$.

$x^2 - x - 20 = 0$

$(x - 5)(x + 4) = 0$

$x = -5$ and $x = 4$

Explain the mistakes that Mnambi made and give the correct solutions.

PB
ES **4** Rhodri thinks of a number between 1 and 10.

He squares the number and then subtracts his original number from the result.

His final answer is 42.

What was Rhodri's original number?

DF
ES **5** A rectangle measures $(x + 1)$ cm by $(x + 2)$ cm.
The area of the rectangle is 72 cm².
What are the dimensions of the rectangle?

$(x + 2)$ cm

$(x + 1)$ cm

PB
ES
6 The diagram shows a rectangle and two trapeziums drawn inside a square of side length 20 cm.

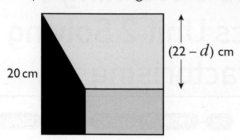

The area of the rectangle is 32 cm² and is given by $(d^2 - 4)$ cm².
Work out the area of each of the trapeziums.

PB
ES
7 This shape is made from two identical right-angled triangles.
The total area of the shape is 135 cm².
Work out the length of the shortest side of one of these triangles.

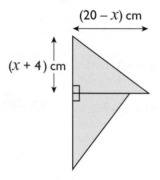

PB
ES
8 The cuboid in the diagram has a total surface area of 246 cm².
Work out the volume of the cuboid.

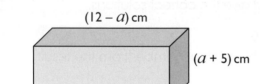

PB
ES
9 What is the area of this right-angled triangle?

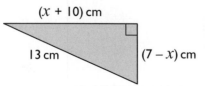

Algebra Strand 5 Working with quadratics Unit 3 Factorising harder quadratics

PS – PRACTISING SKILLS   **DF** – DEVELOPING FLUENCY   **PB** – PROBLEM SOLVING   **ES** – EXAM-STYLE

PS **1** Factorise these.

    a $6x^2 + 2x - 20$

    b $6x^2 - 22x + 20$

    c $6x^2 - 58x - 20$

    d $6x^2 - 26x + 20$

    e $6x^2 - 34x + 20$

    f $6x^2 - 26x - 20$

PS **2** Solve these.

    a $2x^2 + 5x - 3 = 0$

    b $3x^2 - 27 = 0$

    c $3x^2 + 5x = 2$

    d $(2x - 1)^2 = 3x^2 - 2$

PB
ES **3** The diagram shows four identical rectangular tiles placed in a pattern, surrounding a square. The area of each rectangle is $80\,cm^2$.

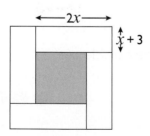

Find the area of the grey square.

DF
ES **4** Factorise $4(x + 2)^2 - 8(x + 2) - 5$.

DF **5** Simplify these.

a $\dfrac{x^2 - 16}{2x^2 - 9x + 4}$

b $\dfrac{x^3 - 9x^2 + 20x}{2x^3 - 6x^2 - 20x}$

c $\dfrac{6x^2 - 2x}{2x^2 - 7x - 4} \div \dfrac{6x^2 + x - 1}{-2x^2 + 9x - 4}$

DF **6** Factorise these.

a $6ac + bd + 3bc + 2ad$

b $6a^3 - 12b^2 - 9ab + 8a^2b$

c $x^4 - 1$

PE **7** A man is four times as old as his son. Five years ago the product of their ages was 234.

a If x is the age of the son, show that $4x^2 - 25x - 209 = 0$.

b Solve $4x^2 - 25x - 209 = 0$ to find their present ages.

PE **8** A stone is dropped down a well. The distance, in metres, the stone has fallen is given by the expression $6t + 5t^2$, where t is the time in seconds.

How long does it take for the stone to reach a depth of 155 metres?

PE **9** The diagram shows a picture inside a frame. The picture is in the shape of a rectangle, 10 cm by 8 cm. The width of the frame is x cm all round the picture. The grey area of the frame is 63 cm².

a Show that $4x^2 + 36x - 63 = 0$.

b Solve $4x^2 + 36x - 63 = 0$ and give the dimensions of the outside of the frame.

PE **10** Here is a right-angled triangle.

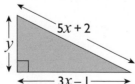

$y = \sqrt{15}$

If all measurements are in centimetres, work out the perimeter of the triangle.

Algebra Strand 5 Working with quadratics Unit 4 The quadratic formula

PS — PRACTISING SKILLS   **DF** — DEVELOPING FLUENCY   **PB** — PROBLEM SOLVING   **ES** — EXAM-STYLE

PS **1** $ax^2 + bx + c = 0$ is the general form of a quadratic equation.
Write down the values of a, b and c for these equations.

a $x^2 + 3x - 7 = 0$ **b** $5x^2 - x + 20 = 0$ **c** $5 - 2x - x^2 = 0$

d $x^2 = 5x + 4$ **e** $5(x - 2x^2) = 9$

PS **2** **i** For each of the quadratic equations in Question 1, state whether
$b^2 - 4ac < 0$, $b^2 - 4ac = 0$ or $b^2 - 4ac > 0$.

ii What can be said about the roots of a quadratic equation when
$b^2 - 4ac < 0$, $b^2 - 4ac = 0$ or $b^2 - 4ac > 0$?

DF **3** Solve each of the quadratic equations in Question 1.

PB
ES **4** An open box has dimensions $5\,$cm by $x\,$cm by $(x + 1.5)\,$cm.
The surface area of the box is $37\,$cm^2.

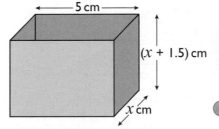

Work out the value of x.

PB
ES **5** The diagram shows a right-angled
triangle. All measurements
are in centimetres.

Work out the area of this triangle.

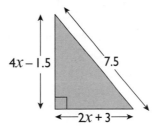

93

DF **6** Solve these.

    a $\dfrac{3}{x} = \dfrac{x-7}{5}$ **b** $\dfrac{2m+3}{m} = \dfrac{1-m}{5}$

    c $\dfrac{n+5}{2n} = \dfrac{n-4}{9}$ **d** $(4w-3)(3w+2) = (5w+2)(2w+1)$

PE
ES **7** The diagram represents a circular path surrounding a circular pond.
The width of the path is 2 metres. The area of the path is a half of the
area of the pond. The average depth of the pond is 1.5 metres.

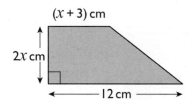

    Work out the volume of water in the pond.

PE
ES **8** Sam walks a distance of 15 km at an average speed of v km/h.
Jane walks the same distance of 15 km at an average speed
of 2 km/h faster than Sam. Jane takes 90 minutes less than Sam.

    Work out Sam's average speed.

PE
ES **9** The diagram shows a trapezium.

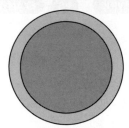

$(x+3)$ cm

$2x$ cm

12 cm

    Work out the perimeter of the trapezium if its area is 30 cm².

PE
ES **10 a** n is an integer. The sum of n and its reciprocal is also an integer.
        Find n.

    b p is an integer. The sum of p and its reciprocal is 2.5. Find p.

    c The sum of a number and its reciprocal is 6. What possible
        number could this be?

Geometry and Measures
Strand 1 Units and scales
Unit 11 Dimensions of formulae

PS — **PRACTISING SKILLS**   **DF** — **DEVELOPING FLUENCY**   **PB** — **PROBLEM SOLVING**   **ES** — **EXAM-STYLE**

DF **1** p, q and r are all lengths.
State whether each of the following are:
lengths   areas   volumes   none of these.

a $pq + qr$ **b** $4p + 3rq$

c $q^2 + r^2$ **d** $\pi r + 4q$

DF **2** m, n and p are all lengths.
State whether each of the following are:
lengths   areas   volumes   none of these.

a $p^2m + m^2n$ **b** $4m - 3p^2$

c $6p^2 + \pi n^2$ **d** $\pi p^3 + 4m^2n$

DF **3** e, f and g are all lengths.
State whether each of the following are:
lengths   areas   volumes   none of these.

a $\dfrac{g}{e} + f$ **b** $\dfrac{4e^2 + 3f^2}{g}$

c $\dfrac{6g^3 + \pi e^3}{f^2}$ **d** $\dfrac{e^3 + 4f^3}{g}$

DF **4** x, y and z are all lengths.
Write down the dimensions of each of the following.

a $\sqrt{(xy)}$ **b** $\sqrt{(x^2 - y^2)}$

c $\dfrac{(xy)^2}{z}$ **d** $\dfrac{\pi yz^2}{\sqrt{(xz)}}$

DF **5** r and h are both lengths.

One of the following expressions represents a volume.
Which one is it?

a $r^2h + \pi rh$

b $\dfrac{3rh^2}{4} - 4r^2\sqrt{h^2}$

c $4^2r^2h - 3^2rh$

d $r^3 + \dfrac{h^3}{h}$

PB **6** A shape is made from joining a hemisphere onto a cylinder.
The radius of both the hemisphere and the cylinder is r cm.
The height of the cylinder is h cm.

a Which one of the following could be the expression for the total volume of the shape?

$\dfrac{2}{3}\pi r^2 + \pi r^2h \qquad \dfrac{2}{3}\pi r^3 + \pi r^2h \qquad \dfrac{2}{3}\pi r^3 + 2\pi rh$

b Give a reason for your answer based on the dimensions of all the expressions.

PB **7** Gareth says that the surface area of the 3D shape he has made is
$rh + 2\pi h + \dfrac{1}{4}r^2$, where r and h are lengths.

a Explain how you know Gareth's expression for what he thinks is the surface area of his 3D shape is incorrect.

b Only one of the terms of Gareth's expression is incorrect, which term is it? And how do you know?

PB **8** Glenda says that the volume of the shape she has made from clay is given by $\pi r^2h + \pi rh^2 + \dfrac{(rh)^2}{rh}$
where r and h are lengths.

Could Glenda's expression possibly be correct? Give a reason for your answer.

PB **9** Harri knows that p represents a length and that r represents an area.
He is given the following formula

$G = \dfrac{1}{2}pr + p^2\sqrt{r}$

Harri needs to decide if the formula he has been given is going to calculate a length, and area or a volume.

Explain to Harri how you know what this formula could be used to calculate (a length, an area or a volume) giving detailed reasons for your answer.

Geometry and Measures
Strand 1 Units and scales
Unit 12 Working with compound units

PS – PRACTISING SKILLS   **DF** – DEVELOPING FLUENCY   **PB** – PROBLEM SOLVING   **ES** – EXAM-STYLE

PS
ES **1** Grass seed is sold in three sizes of box.
Which size of box is the best value for money?

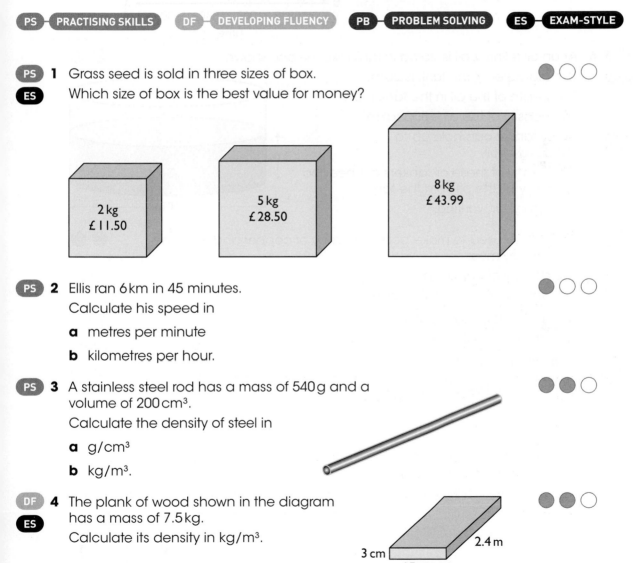

2 kg
£11.50

5 kg
£28.50

8 kg
£43.99

PS **2** Ellis ran 6 km in 45 minutes.
Calculate his speed in

a metres per minute

b kilometres per hour.

PS **3** A stainless steel rod has a mass of 540 g and a
volume of 200 cm³.
Calculate the density of steel in

a g/cm³

b kg/m³.

DF
ES **4** The plank of wood shown in the diagram
has a mass of 7.5 kg.
Calculate its density in kg/m³.

2.4 m

3 cm

15 cm

DF **ES** **5** The graph shows Myra's car journey from her home to her mother's house.

Work out the average speed of this journey.

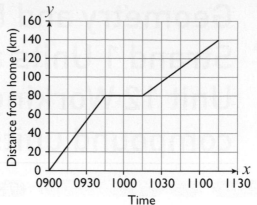

PB **ES** **6** At an oil refinery, oil is stored in tanks like the one shown.

The diameter of the tank is 20 m.

The depth of the oil in the tank is 5 m.

The density of the oil is 800 kg/m³.

An oil tanker can hold up to 50 000 kg of oil.

How many of these oil tankers are needed to empty all the oil from the tank?

Show all your working.

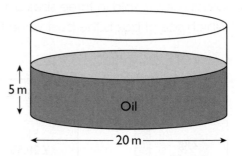

PB **7** The bronze used to make bells is an alloy of copper and tin in the ratio 4 : 1 by mass.

The density of copper is 8.96 g/cm³.

The density of tin is 7.365 g/cm³.

a A bell has a mass of 2 tonnes. Work out

  i the mass of copper

  ii the mass of tin.

b Calculate the density of the bronze.

Geometry and Measures
Strand 2 Properties of shapes
Unit 9 Congruent triangles and proof

PS — **PRACTISING SKILLS**   **DF** — **DEVELOPING FLUENCY**   **PB** — **PROBLEM SOLVING**   **ES** — **EXAM-STYLE**

PS **1** State whether the triangles in each pair are congruent.
If they are, give a reason.

a

5 cm   6 cm   6 cm   5 cm
5 cm   5 cm

b

5 cm   6 cm   5 cm   5 cm
5 cm   6 cm

c
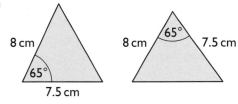

8 cm   8 cm   65°   7.5 cm
65°
7.5 cm

d
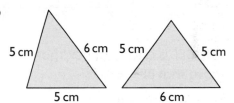

12 cm   9 cm   9 cm   12 cm
45°   45°

e
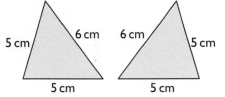

15 cm
15 cm   5 cm
5 cm

f
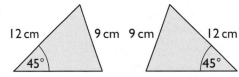

70°   55°   70°   55°

g
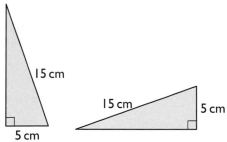

5 cm
54°   75°

75°   54°
5 cm

h
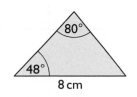

80°
48°   80°   48°
8 cm   8 cm

99

DF **2** The diagram shows a parallelogram, PQRS.
ES Prove that triangle PRS and triangle PQR are congruent.

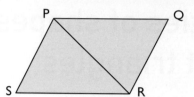

DF **3** Explain why triangles PQR and XYZ are not congruent.
ES

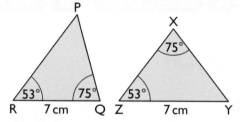

PB **4** ABCDEF is a regular hexagon.
ES Prove that BF = BD.

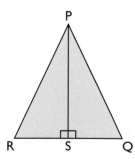

DF **5** PQR is an isosceles triangle with PQ = PR.
ES PS bisects the angle at P and the side RQ.
Prove that triangles PQS and PSR are congruent.

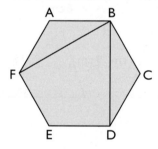

DF

6 ABCDE is a regular pentagon.
BFGC is a rectangle.
Prove that triangles ABF and
DCG are congruent.

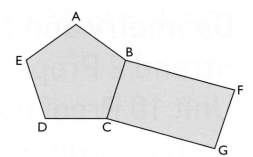

PE

7 In this diagram
AD = CD
$\angle A = \angle C = 90°$
Prove that DB bisects $\angle ABC$.

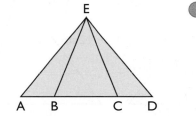

PE

8 In triangle EAD
EA = ED
$\angle AEB = \angle CED$.
Explain why AB = CD.

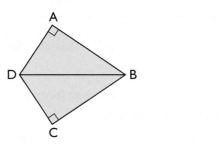

PB

9 ABCE is an isosceles trapezium.
BC = BD
AB is parallel to EDC.
ABDE is a parallelogram
Prove that triangles ABD and ADE
are congruent.
Write down any assumptions you
have made.

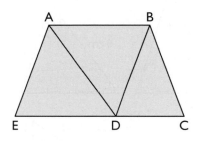

PB

10 ABC is a right-angled
triangle.
ABED and ACFG are
squares.
Prove that triangles
ABG and ACD are
congruent.

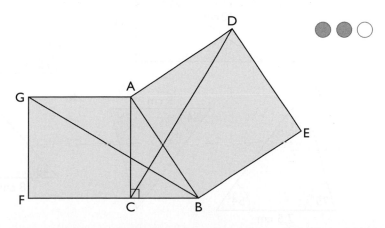

Geometry and Measures
Strand 2 Properties of shapes
Unit 10 Proof using similar and congruent triangles

PS PRACTISING SKILLS   **DF** DEVELOPING FLUENCY   **PB** PROBLEM SOLVING   **ES** EXAM-STYLE

PS **1** For each part, state whether the two triangles are similar or congruent. ●●○
Give a reasons for each answer.

a

12 cm   10 cm
5 cm   6 cm
5 cm   5 cm   10 cm

b

5 cm   6 cm   7.5 cm   7.5 cm
5 cm   9 cm

c
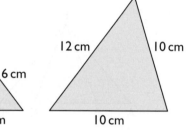

6 cm   55°   6 cm   5 cm
55°
5 cm

d
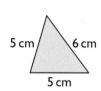

12 cm   9 cm   8 cm   6 cm
45°   45°

e
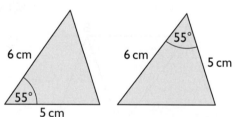

5 cm   10 cm   6 cm
3 cm

f
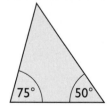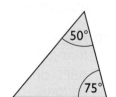

50°
75°   50°   75°

g
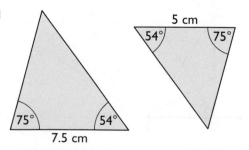

5 cm
54°   75°
75°   54°
7.5 cm

h
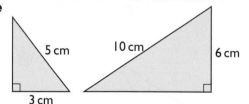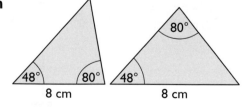

80°
48°   80°   48°
8 cm   8 cm

102

DF **2** ABD and ACE are straight lines.
BC is parallel to DE.
Prove that triangles ABC and ADE are similar.

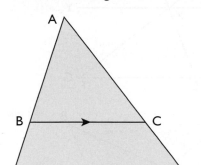

DF **3** AB is parallel to PQ.
Prove that triangles ABX and PQX are similar.

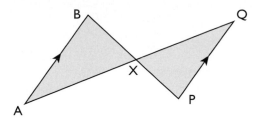

DF
ES **4** Show that triangle DEF is similar to triangle GHJ.

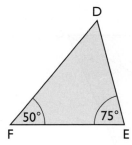

PB
ES **5** PQRS, WXY and DEFG are parallel lines.
RX = XE
Prove that triangles QRX and EFX
are congruent.

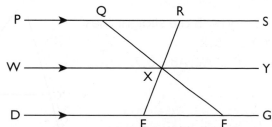

PB
ES
6 PQRS, WXY and DEF are parallel lines.

RX:XE = 2:3

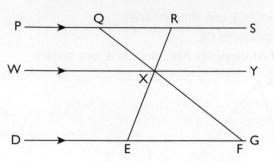

a Prove that triangles QRX and EFX are similar.

b How many times longer is FQ than QX?

PB
ES
7 ABCD is a parallelogram.

The diagonals intersect at X.

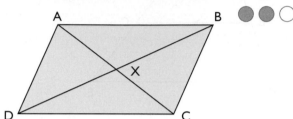

a Prove that triangles AXD and BXC are congruent.

b Show that X is the mid-point of AC and BD.

PB
ES
8 Show that PQ is parallel to RS.

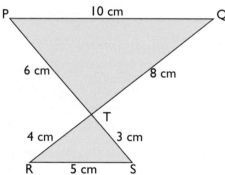

PB
9 PQRT and UVST are parallelograms.
PUT, TSR and TVQ are straight lines.

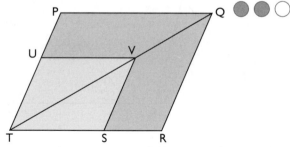

a Prove that triangle UVT is similar to triangle PQT.

b Given that PU:UT = 2:3, find the value of QV:QT.

PB
10 XZBC is a parallelogram.
AXC and AYB are straight lines.
AX:XC = 5:2.
Show that AY:AB = 5:7.

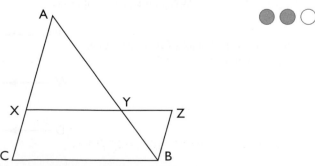

Geometry and Measures Strand 2 Properties of shapes Unit 11 Circle theorems

PS — **PRACTISING SKILLS**   DF — DEVELOPING FLUENCY   PB — **PROBLEM SOLVING**   ES — **EXAM-STYLE**

PS **1** Find the size of the angle marked with a letter in each diagram. Give a reason for each of your answers.

a
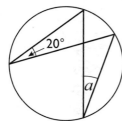

b
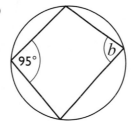

c
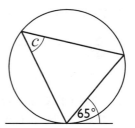

PS **2** Each circle in this question has a centre O. Find the size of the angle marked with a letter. Give a reason for each of your answers.

a
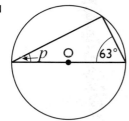

b
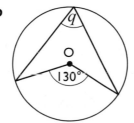

c
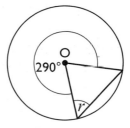

DF
ES **3** The diagram shows a circle centre O. PA and PB are tangents to the circle.

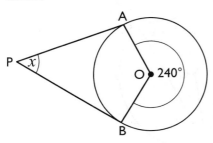

Find the size of the angle marked x.

PB
ES
4 P, Q, R and S are points on the circumference of a circle centre O.
Angle PRQ = 50°.

Find the size of the angle marked y. Give reasons for each stage of your working.

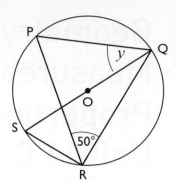

DF
ES
5 D, E and F are points on the circumference of a circle centre O.
Angle DOF = 140°.

Work out the size of the angle marked g. Give reasons for each stage of your working.

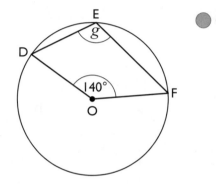

PB
ES
6 TP and TR are tangents to the circle centre O.

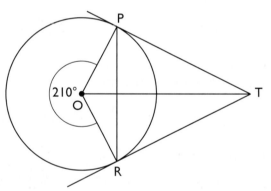

Find the size of angle PTR. Give reasons for each stage of your working.

PB
ES
7 A, B and C are points on the circle centre O. Angle ABC is $x°$. TA and TC are tangents to the circle.

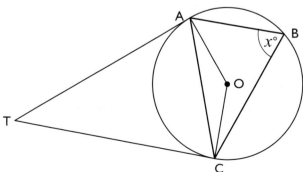

Prove that TA = TC.

PB
ES

8 B, C, D and E are points on the circumference of the circle centre O. EB is parallel to DC. XD is a tangent to the circle at D.

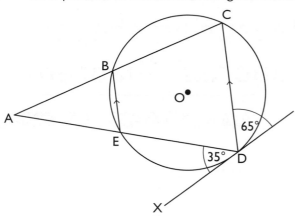

Using the information on the diagram prove that triangle ABE is isosceles.

PB
ES

9 AB, BC and CA are tangents to the circle at P, Q and R respectively. Angle B = $2x°$. Angle C = $2y°$.

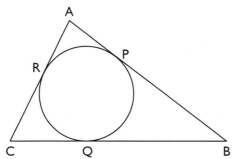

Find an expression in terms of x and y for the size of angle PQR.

PB
ES

10 The circle centre O has a radius of 7 cm. The circle centre P has a radius of 10 cm. AB is a tangent to both circles.

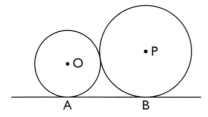

a Find the length of AB.

b What assumptions have you made in your solution?

Geometry and Measures
Strand 3 Measuring shapes
Unit 5 Pythagoras' Theorem

PS — PRACTISING SKILLS   **DF** — DEVELOPING FLUENCY   **PB** — PROBLEM SOLVING   **ES** — EXAM-STYLE

PS **1** Work out the length of the hypotenuse in each triangle.
Give your answers correct to 1 decimal place.

a

8 cm

6 cm

b

6 cm

4 cm

c

3 cm   4.5 cm

PS **2** Work out the length of the unknown side in each triangle.
Give your answer correct to 2 decimal places.

a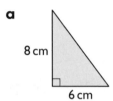

6 cm   8 cm

b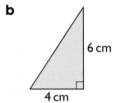

6 cm

4 cm

c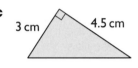

3 cm

4.5 cm

DF **3** Without using a calculator, work out the length of the unknown side
in each triangle.

a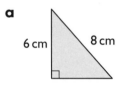

√5 cm

√11 cm

b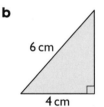

√35 cm

√10 cm

c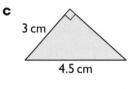

√44 cm

12 cm

DF **4** Which of the three triangles are right-angled triangles?
Explain your answer.

a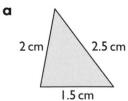

2 cm   2.5 cm

1.5 cm

b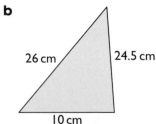

26 cm   24.5 cm

10 cm

c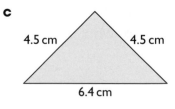

4.5 cm   4.5 cm

6.4 cm

DF **ES** **5** ABCD is a rectangle.
Work out the length of the diagonal BD.
Give your answer correct to 3 significant figures.

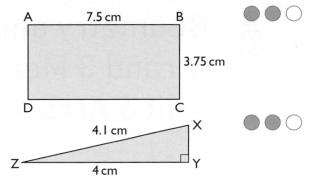

DF **6** For triangle XYZ, work out

   a the perimeter

   b the area.

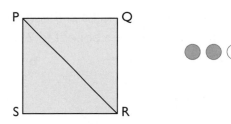

DF **ES** **7** PQRS is a square. The diagonal is 16 cm.
Work out the perimeter of the square.
Give your answer correct to 3 significant figures.

PB **8** A square is drawn with its vertices on the circumference of a circle.
The diagonal of the square is 8 cm.
Work out the area of the shaded part of the diagram, giving your answer correct to 3 significant figures.

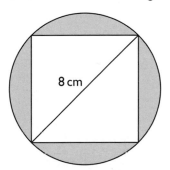

PB **ES** **9** Calculate the area of the field shown in this diagram.
Give your answer in hectares to 3 significant figures.
(1 hectare = 10 000 m²)

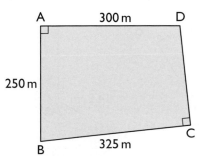

Geometry and Measures
Strand 3 Measuring shapes
Unit 6 Arcs and sectors

PS – **PRACTISING SKILLS**   **DF** – **DEVELOPING FLUENCY**   **PB** – **PROBLEM SOLVING**   **ES** – **EXAM-STYLE**

PS **1** Calculate the lengths of these arcs.
Give your answers correct to 2 decimal places.   ●●○

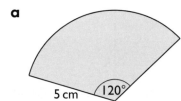

a 5 cm 120°

b 7 cm

c 15 cm 44°

PS **2** Calculate the areas of these sectors.
Give your answers correct to 1 decimal place.   ●●○

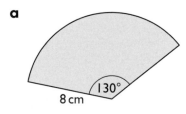 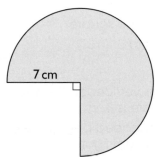 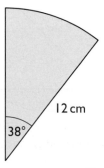

a 8 cm 130°

b 10 cm

c 12 cm 38°

PS **3** Work out the perimeter and area of each shape.
Give your answers correct to 3 significant figures.   ●●○

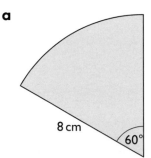 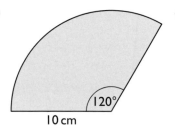 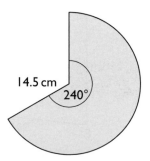

a 8 cm 60°

b 10 cm 120°

c 14.5 cm 240°

110

DF **4** The shaded part of this diagram shows the throwing area of a sports field.

Calculate the area.

Give your answer to the nearest whole number.

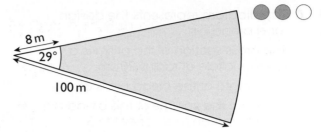

DF **5** A sector has a radius of 7.5 cm and an area of 25π cm².

Calculate the angle at the centre.

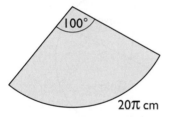

DF **6** A sector arc has length of 20π cm and an angle of 100°.

Calculate the radius of the sector.

PB **7** The arc length of a sector is the same as its radius.

ES What is the angle at the centre?

Give your answer correct to 3 significant figures.

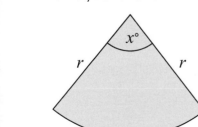

PB
ES

8 The diagram represents the design for a bread bin.

The cross-section of the prism is a quarter circle of radius 20 cm.

The length of the bread bin is 35 cm.

Work out the volume of this bread bin, giving your answer correct to 3 significant figures.

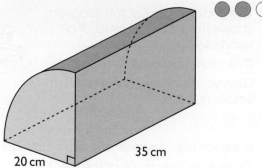

35 cm

20 cm

PB
ES

9 The diagram represents the plan for a flower bed.

The flower bed is the region between 2 semicircles. The semicircles have the same centre, S.

Percy wants to put edging strips along each edge of the flower bed.

He has 15 lengths of edging strip. Each length is 1.5 m.

Does Percy have enough edging strip?

Show your working.

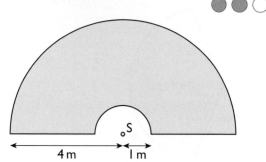

S

4 m   1 m

PB
ES

10 The diagram shows the design for a brooch. The brooch has diameter 2.5 cm and will be made from three different metals.

The area of the gold, silver and copper sectors are in the ratio 4 : 3 : 1.

Work out the total area of the silver sectors, giving your answer correct to 1 decimal place.

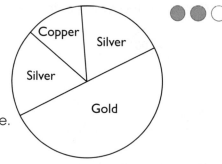

Copper

Silver

Silver

Gold

DF
ES

11 Work out the area that is shaded.

Give your answer in terms of π.

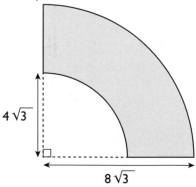

$4\sqrt{3}$

$8\sqrt{3}$

Geometry and Measures
Strand 3 Measuring shapes
Unit 7 The cosine rule

PS PRACTISING SKILLS　　DF DEVELOPING FLUENCY　　PB PROBLEM SOLVING　　ES EXAM-STYLE

PS **1** Calculate the length of the marked with a letter in each side of these triangles. Give your answers correct to three significant figures.

a
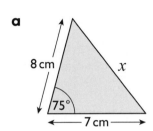
8 cm
x
75°
7 cm

b

5 cm 35° 8 cm
y

c

z
10 cm
120°
4 cm

PS **ES** **2** PQR is a triangle.

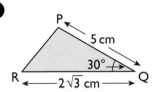
P
5 cm
30°
R
$2\sqrt{3}$ cm
Q

Work out the length of the side PR. Give your answer in surd form.

PS **3** Calculate the size of the angles marked with a letter in these diagrams. Give your answers correct to one decimal place.

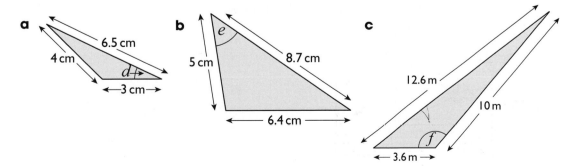

a
6.5 cm
4 cm
d
3 cm

b
e
5 cm
8.7 cm
6.4 cm

c
12.6 m
10 m
f
3.6 m

113

DF **ES** **4** Ipswich is 20 miles due east of Sudbury. Colchester is 18.5 miles on a bearing of 230° from Ipswich.

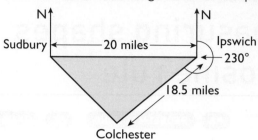

Find the distance of Sudbury from Colchester.

DF **ES** **5** The perimeter of this isosceles triangle is 25 cm. The shortest side QR is 7 cm.

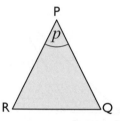

Find the size of angle p.

DF **ES** **6** Here is triangle ABC. Angle A is 40°. $b = 9.8$ cm, $c = 7.2$ cm. Find the length of BC.

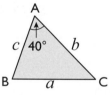

PB **ES** **7** A boat delivers supplies to two oil rigs. The boat sails from the harbour, H. It sails in a straight line from H to R, then from R to S then back to H. The bearing of R from H is 050°. The bearing of S from H is 120°. R is 20 km from H. S is 15 km from H.

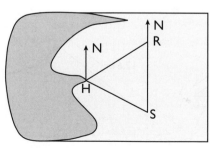

Work out the total distance the boat travels. Give your answer correct to one decimal place.

PS
ES

8 A surveyor measures a farmer's field and puts the measurements on this sketch.

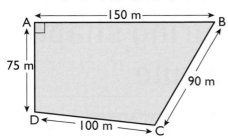

Find the size of angle BCD. Give your answer correct to one decimal place.

PB
ES

9 A builder ropes off the outline of a triangular plot of ground. PQ = 45 m, PR = 60 m and angle QPR = 75°.

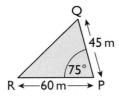

What is the shortest length of rope the builder needs? Give your answer to the nearest metre.

PB
ES

10 The diagram shows the roof of a house. There needs to be at least 2 m from the top of the roof at C to the base of the roof AB.

Does this roof meet these requirements? You must show all your working.

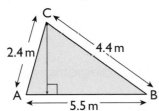

Geometry and Measures
Strand 3 Measuring shapes
Unit 8 The sine rule

PS PRACTISING SKILLS   **DF** DEVELOPING FLUENCY   **PB** PROBLEM SOLVING   **ES** EXAM-STYLE

PS **1** Calculate the length of the side marked with a letter in each of these triangles. Give your answers correct to three significant figures.

a

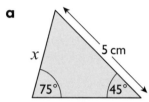

x 5 cm 75° 45°

b

10 cm 20° 120° y

c

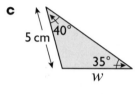

5 cm 40° 35° w

PS **2** PQR is a triangle.

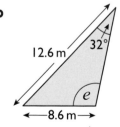

Q 105° 25° P 4.5 m R

Work out the length of the side PQ. Give your answer correct to two decimal places.

PS **3** Calculate the size of the angles marked with a letter in these diagrams. Give your answers correct to one decimal place.

a

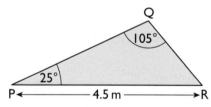

4.2 cm 6.9 cm 80° d

b

12.6 m 32° e 8.6 m

c

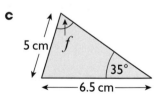

5 cm f 35° 6.5 cm

DF ES **4** A castle is on a bearing of 145° from a church. The church is due
west of a folly. The castle is 8 miles on a bearing of 240° from the folly.

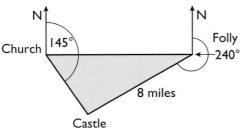

Find the distance of the folly from the church.

DF ES **5** In triangle PQR, PQ = 12.5 cm, Angle Q = 40° and PR = 10 cm.

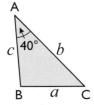

Find two possible values for the size of angle R.

PS ES **6** Here is triangle ABC. Angle A is 40°, b = 9.8 cm, c = 7.2 cm.
Find the area of the triangle ABC.

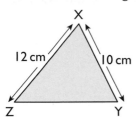

DF ES **7** Triangle XYZ has an area of 40 cm². XY = 10 cm, XZ = 12 cm.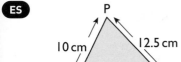
Find the size of angle X.

PB **ES** **8** A surveyor measures a farmer's field and puts the measurements on this sketch.

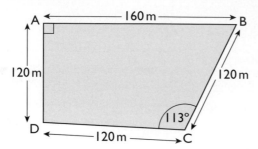

Find the area of the field. Give your answer correct to three significant figures.

PB **ES** **9** Osian is planning an orienteering trip. He is going to walk from P to Q to R and then back to P. Q is on a bearing of 050° from P. R is on a bearing of 160° from Q and 110° from P. PQ = 7.5 km.

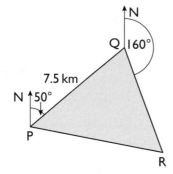

How far is Osian planning to walk? Give your answer correct to three significant figures.

PB **ES** **10** The diagram shows the cross section of a large tent. There needs to be at least 3.5 m from the top of the tent at C to the base of the tent AB.

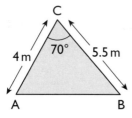

Does this tent meet these requirements? You must show all your working.

Geometry and Measures Strand 4
Construction Unit 4 Loci

 **PS** — PRACTISING SKILLS   **DF** — DEVELOPING FLUENCY   **PB** — PROBLEM SOLVING   **ES** — EXAM-STYLE

PS **1** Draw a co-ordinate grid on 2 mm graph paper.
Draw the x-axis from –6 to 6.
Draw the y-axis from –5 to 7.
Draw the locus of the points that are

   a 4 cm from (1, 1)

   b 2 cm from the line joining (–3, 3) and (–3, –2)

   c the same distance from the points (1, 5) and (5, 1)

   d the same distance from the lines joining (–4, 4) to (0, –4) and (0, 4) to (–4, –4).

PB **2** The diagram shows Fflur's garden.
Fflur wants to plant a new tree in her garden.
The tree will be planted:

   • nearer to RQ than RS

   • more than 10 m from PS

   • less than 8 m from Q.

   a Draw the diagram accurately, using a scale of 1 cm = 2 m.

   b Shade the region where Fflur could plant her new tree.

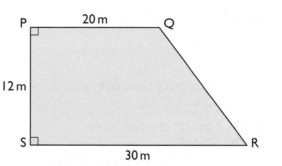

PB **3** The diagram shows the positions of Colchester and Ipswich.
Ipswich is 18 miles north east of Colchester.
A company want to build a new hotel such that

   • it is nearer Ipswich than Colchester

   • it is less than 12 miles from Colchester.

   a Draw the diagram accurately, using a scale of 1 cm = 2 miles.

   b Shade the region where the hotel could be built.

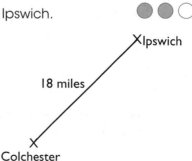

PB **4** The diagram shows a car park that measures 75m by 55m.
Cars must not be parked within 20m of W or within 15m of XY.

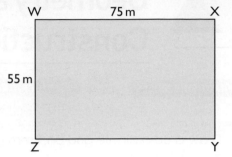

a Draw the car park accurately, using a scale of 1cm = 10m.

b Shade the region where the cars should not be parked.

DF **ES** **5** PQRS is a square piece of card placed on a straight line.

The card is first rotated 90° clockwise about R.
It is then rotated 90° clockwise about Q.
Finally it is rotated 90° clockwise about P.
Draw the locus of the vertex S.

PB **ES** **6** In the diagram:

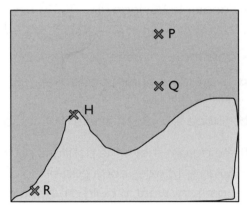

- P and Q are buoys.
  P is 750m due North of Q and Q is 1km NE of H.

- H is 1km on a bearing of 020° from R.

  Ewan has to steer his boat along a course from port R between the buoys at P and Q. He must stay at least 300m away from H.

  He wants to sail due North from R and then onto a course on the perpendicular bisector of P and Q.

a Draw an accurate diagram of Ewan's boat trip, using a scale of 1cm = 100m.

b Will he pass too close to H?
Explain your answer.

Geometry and Measures
Strand 5 Transformations
Unit 7 Similarity

PS — **PRACTISING SKILLS**   **DF** — **DEVELOPING FLUENCY**   **PB** — **PROBLEM SOLVING**   **ES** — **EXAM-STYLE**

PS **1** Work out the lettered lengths in each pair of similar triangles. ●●○

a

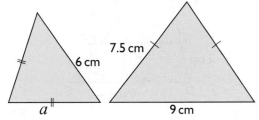

b

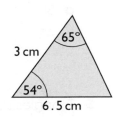

c

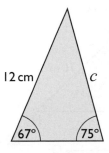

d

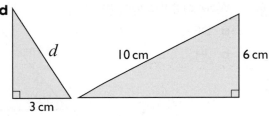

PS **2** XYZ and PQR are two similar triangles. Work out the length of

a XY

b PR.

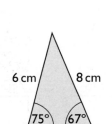

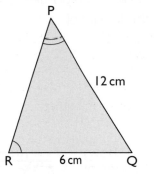

DF **3** Work out the lettered lengths in each pair of similar shapes. ●●○

a

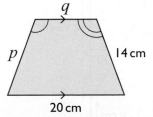

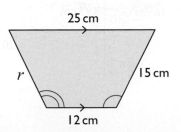

b

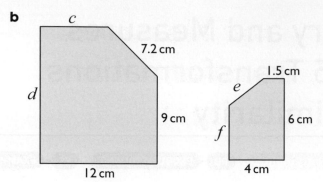

DF **ES** **4** ABC and ADE are two similar triangles.
BC is parallel to DE.
Work out the length of

a BC

b AE.

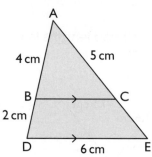

DF **ES** **5** Triangles DEF and HGJ are similar.
Work out the length of

a DE

b JH.

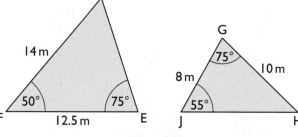

DF **ES** **6** In this diagram, PQ is parallel to RS.
Work out the length of

a RT

b PT.

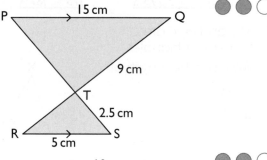

PB **ES** **7** The diagram shows a set of supports of two sizes made to support shelves.
Work out the value of

a x

b y.

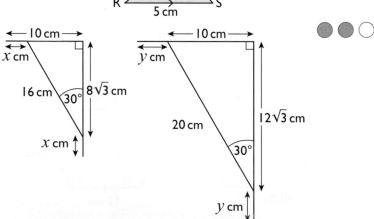

Geometry and Measures
Strand 5 Transformations
Unit 8 Trigonometry

PS PRACTISING SKILLS **DF** DEVELOPING FLUENCY **PB** PROBLEM SOLVING **ES** EXAM-STYLE

PS **1** Work out the length of the lettered side in each right-angled triangle.
Give your answers correct to 1 decimal place.

a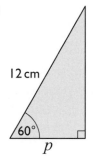
12 cm
60°
p

b
q
50°
8 cm

c
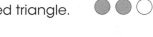
r
55°
15 cm

PS **2** For each triangle, work out the value of θ.
Give your answer correct to 1 decimal place.

a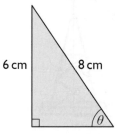
6 cm   8 cm
θ

b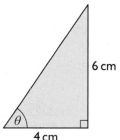
6 cm
θ
4 cm

c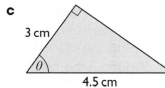
3 cm
θ
4.5 cm

PS **3** Work out the length of the lettered side in each right-angled triangle.
Give your answers correct to 2 decimal places.

a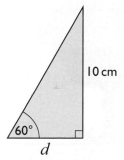
10 cm
60°
d

b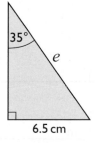
35°
e
6.5 cm

c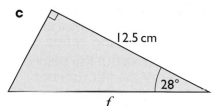
12.5 cm
28°
f

123

DF **ES** **4** Work out the perpendicular height h of this triangle.

Give your answer correct to 3 significant figures.

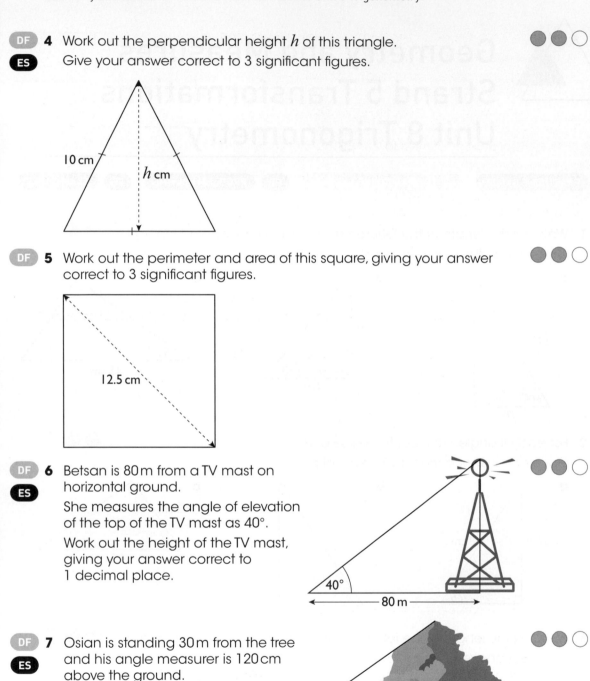

10 cm

h cm

DF **5** Work out the perimeter and area of this square, giving your answer correct to 3 significant figures.

12.5 cm

DF **ES** **6** Betsan is 80 m from a TV mast on horizontal ground.

She measures the angle of elevation of the top of the TV mast as 40°.

Work out the height of the TV mast, giving your answer correct to 1 decimal place.

40°

80 m

DF **ES** **7** Osian is standing 30 m from the tree and his angle measurer is 120 cm above the ground.

He measures the angle of elevation to the top of tree as 35°.

Work out the height of the tree, correct to 3 significant figures.

35°

120 cm

30 m

8 The diagram shows a framework made from five rods.

The rectangle has a length of 12 m.

The diagonal makes an angle of 25° with the base of the rectangle.

Work out the total length of the five rods in the framework.

Give your answer correct to 3 significant figures.

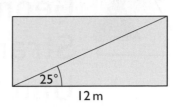

9 The longest diagonal of a rhombus is 10 cm.

This diagonal makes an angle of 30° with the base of the rhombus.

Work out the perimeter of the rhombus, giving your answer correct to 3 significant figures.

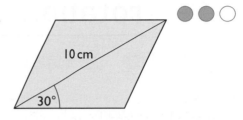

10 Alfie takes his boat to check two offshore windmills at W and M.

He leaves the harbour H and travels due East for 12 km to W and then 5 km due North to M.

On what bearing must he travel to get directly back to H?

Give your answer to the nearest degree.

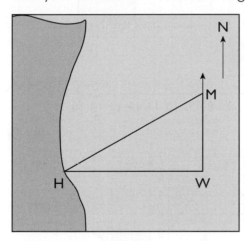

11 Kirsty wants to find the width of a river.

She stands at the top of the tower, T.
The base of the tower is at A.

ABC is a straight line.

Angle TAB is a right angle.

The angle of depression of:

- B from T is 40°

- C from T is 30°.

The base of the tower is 100 m from B.

Work out the width of the river.

Give your answer correct to 3 significant figures.

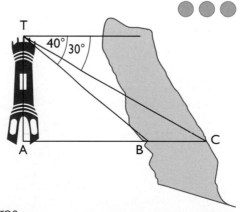

Geometry and Measures
Strand 5 Transformations
Unit 9 Finding centres of rotation

PS — **PRACTISING SKILLS**   **DF** — **DEVELOPING FLUENCY**   **PB** — **PROBLEM SOLVING**   **ES** — **EXAM-STYLE**

PS **1** Copy the diagram. Write down the centre and angle of rotation for

a A → B

b A → C

c A → D

d A → E.

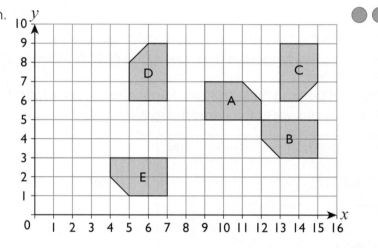

PS **2** Write down the centre and angle of rotation that transforms triangle P onto

a triangle A

b triangle B

c triangle C.

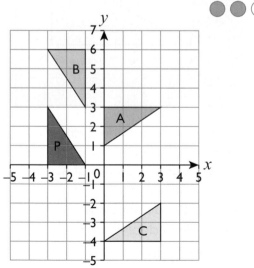

DF **3** Look at the diagram in question **2**. Describe fully the rotations that map

    a triangle A onto triangle C

    b triangle B onto triangle A

    c triangle C onto triangle P

    d triangle B onto triangle C.

DF **4** **a** Describe fully the rotations
that map shape S to

    i shape A

    ii shape B

    iii shape C.

PB   **b** Explain why shape D is not
a rotation of shape S.

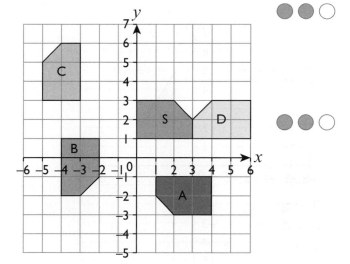

PB **5** **a** Reflect triangle P in the line $x = -2$. Label the new triangle Q.

ES   **b** Reflect triangle Q in the line $y = 1$. Label the new triangle R.

    c Describe fully the single transformation that maps triangle P
directly to triangle R.

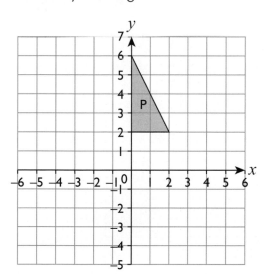

PB
ES

6 **a** Reflect triangle T in the line $x = 0$. Label the new triangle U.

b Translate triangle U by the vector $\begin{pmatrix} 4 \\ -2 \end{pmatrix}$. Label the new triangle V.

c Reflect triangle V in the line $y = -1$. Label the new triangle W.

d Describe fully the single transformation that maps triangle T directly to triangle W.

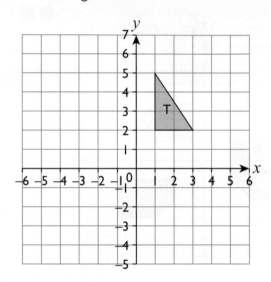

PB
ES

7 Shape P is reflected in the line with equation $y = x + 1$ to give shape Q.
Shape Q is reflected in the line $y = x - 2$ to give shape R.
Describe fully the single transformation that maps shape R directly to shape P.

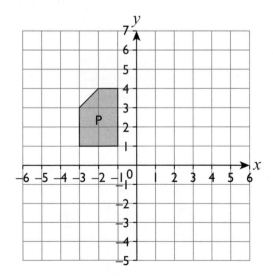

Geometry and Measures
Strand 5 Transformations
Unit 10 Enlargement with negative scale factors

PS – PRACTISING SKILLS   **DF** – DEVELOPING FLUENCY   **PB** – PROBLEM SOLVING   **ES** – EXAM-STYLE

PS
ES

1 Triangle A is drawn on a coordinate grid. Describe fully the single transformation which maps triangle A onto triangle B.

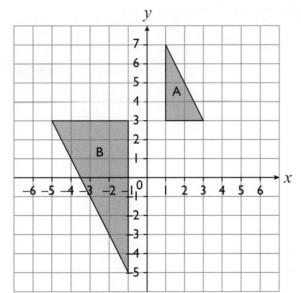

PS **2** Triangle C is drawn on a coordinate grid. Describe fully the single
ES transformation which maps triangle C onto triangle D.

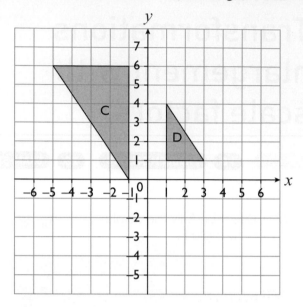

DF **3** Enlarge triangle A with

ES **a** scale factor –2, centre (0, 0)

b scale factor –½, centre (–2, 1).

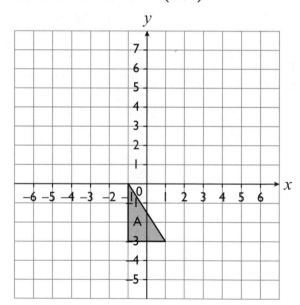

DF **4** Look at the diagram.

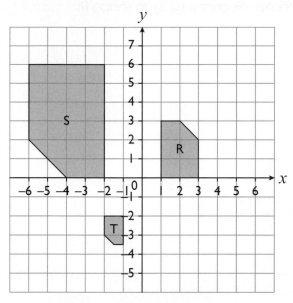

a Describe the single transformation that maps R onto S.

b Describe the single transformation that maps R onto T.

PB **5** A shape, F, is drawn on a coordinate grid. The shape is rotated 180°
ES about the origin.

Describe a different single transformation that can replace this rotation.

PB **6** A shape G is drawn on a coordinate grid. The shape is reflected
ES in the line $x = a$. It is then reflected in the line $y = b$.

Describe two different single transformations that can replace these two reflections.

DF **ES**

7 The shape P is enlarged with scale factor –3, centre (0, 0), to shape Q.
The shape Q is enlarged with scale factor –½, centre (0, 3), to shape R.

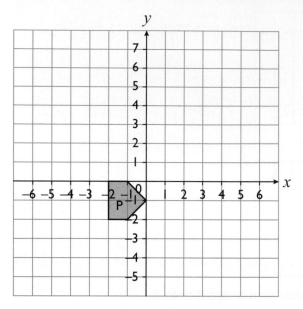

a Draw these enlargements on a coordinate grid.

b Write down the single transformation that takes P directly to R.

Geometry and Measures
Strand 5 Transformations
Unit 11 Trigonometry and
Pythagoras' Theorem in 2D
and 3D

PS — **PRACTISING SKILLS**   **DF** — **DEVELOPING FLUENCY**   **PB** — **PROBLEM SOLVING**   **ES** — **EXAM-STYLE**

PS
ES
1 Here is a cuboid. The cuboid has length 12 cm, width 5 cm and height 6 cm.

● ● ●

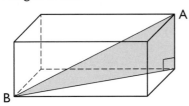

a Work out the length of the diagonal AB.

b Work out the angle AB makes with the base of the cuboid.

PB
ES
2 A stirrer used to stir paint sticks 10 cm out of a paint tin. The tin of paint is 30 cm tall and is a cylinder of radius 8 cm.

● ● ●

a Work out the length of the stirrer.

b What angle does the stirrer make with the base of the tin?

DF
ES
3 Here is a cuboid. It has a length of 12 cm, a width of 6 cm and a height of 4 cm. The vertices of the grey triangle are on the midpoints of three of the edges of the cuboid.

● ● ●

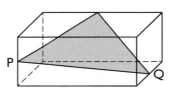

a Work out the perimeter of the grey triangle.

b Work out the angle that PQ makes with the base of the cuboid.

PB
ES **4** David wants to fit a long stick into a box which is in the shape of a cuboid. The length of the box is 0.9m, the width is 30cm and the height is 30m.

    a What is the longest stick that will fit into the box?

    b What is the angle the longest stick will make with the base of the box?

PB
ES **5** Here is a sketch of a grain silo. The grain silo is made from a cylinder and a cone of radius 3m.
The height of the cylinder is 8m.
The height of the cone is 4m.

    Work out the size of the obtuse angle that the edge of the cone makes with the edge of the cylinder.

DF **6** Here is a diagram of a cold frame.
The cold frame is in the shape of a right-angled triangular prism.
A straight piece of metal joins P to Q to strengthen the frame.

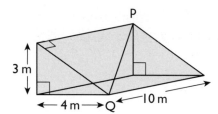

    a Find the length of the piece of metal PQ.

    b Find the angle that PQ makes with the base of the cold frame.

DF **7** Here is a pyramid. It has a square base of side 10cm and a vertical height of 12cm.

    a Work out the angle the edge of a triangular face makes with the base of the pyramid.

    b Work out the angle a triangular face makes with the base of the pyramid.

PB **8**
ES

Here is a cuboid. The length is 15 cm. The width is 8 cm.
The height is 6 cm.

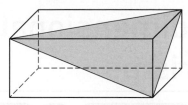

Work out the area of the grey triangle.

PB **9**
ES

Raj is running a TV cable across his bedroom. The cable follows the
black line on the diagram. The room is 4 m long, 3 m wide and 2.5 m high.

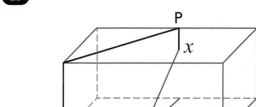

P is halfway along the length of one wall. Q is halfway along another wall.
X is the point where the TV is to be placed. Raj wants the angle that
XQ makes with the floor of the room to be 35°.

Work out the length of TV cable Raj needs. You must show all
your working.

PB **10**
ES

Here is the plan of design for the roof of a conservatory. The roof
is in the shape of an octagonal pyramid. The base of the roof is
a regular octagon of side 1 m. The height of the roof is 0.6 m. The
angle each face makes with the base of the roof has to be more
than 30°.

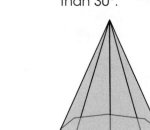

Does this design match the requirements? You must show how you
reach your conclusion.

Geometry and Measures Strand 6 Three-dimensional shapes Unit 5 Prisms

PS — **PRACTISING SKILLS**   **DF** — **DEVELOPING FLUENCY**   **PB** — **PROBLEM SOLVING**   **ES** — **EXAM-STYLE**

PS **1** Here are some prisms. Find their volume. ● ○ ○

a

20 cm² 5 cm

b

15 cm² 6 cm

c

12 cm² 4 cm

PS **2** Here are some prisms. Find their total surface area. ● ○ ○

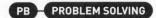
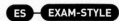

a

2 cm 4 cm 3 cm

b

5 cm 3 cm 4 cm 6 cm

c

3 cm 5 cm 5 cm 4 cm 9 cm 5 cm

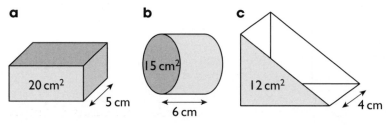

PS **3** Here is a cylinder. ● ○ ○

ES **a** Find the volume of the cylinder.

3 cm ← 8 cm →

b Find the total surface area of the cylinder.

DF **4** Answer these. ● ○ ○

a A hexagonal prism has a cross-sectional area of 35 cm² and a length of 5 cm. Find the volume of the hexagonal prism.

b A cylinder has a volume 1 litre. The area of the circular base is 50 cm². Find the height of the cylinder.

c An octagonal prism has a volume of 24 cm³. The length of the prism is 3 cm. Find the area of the base of the prism.

5 Here is a sketch of Fred's shed. It is in the shape of a pentagonal prism. Fred is going to paint the 6 outside faces of the shed. 1 litre of the paint he uses covers 15 m².

How many litres of paint does he need?

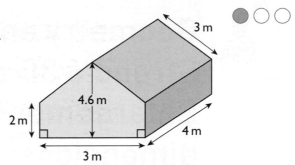

6 Siân makes a plant pot holder for her garden from a cylindrical block of wood. The cylinder has a diameter of 30 cm and a height of 30 cm. Siân cuts a hole with radius 10 cm to a depth of 20 cm into the cylinder.

What volume of wood is left from the original cylinder?

7 Susi is going to grow vegetables in a container in her garden. The container is in the shape of a prism. The ends of the prism are trapeziums.

Susi plans to fill the container completely with compost to a depth of 60 cm. Compost is sold in 65 litre bags.

How many bags of compost will Susi need to buy?

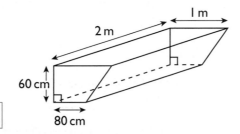

| 1 m³ = 1000 litres |

8 Rhodri has a tank in his garden to store heating oil. The tank is in the shape of a square prism. The tank measures 60 cm by 1.2 m by 1.2 m. The level of oil in the tank is 30 cm from the bottom. Rhodri orders 700 litres of heating oil.

Will there be enough room in the oil tank for all the oil? You must explain your answer.

9 A can of baked beans has a height of 10 cm and a radius of 3.7 cm. The average space needed for one baked bean is 0.2 cm³.

Estimate the number of baked beans in the tin.

10 Zigi has a swimming pool in the shape of a cylinder. The swimming pool has a diameter of 1.2 m. The height of the swimming pool is 90 cm. Zigi empties the swimming pool at a rate of 5 litres of water per minute. She starts emptying the pool at 8.30 a.m.

At what time will the swimming pool be completely empty?

Geometry and Measures
Strand 6 3D shapes Unit 6
Enlargement in 2 and 3
dimensions

PS — **PRACTISING SKILLS**   **DF** — **DEVELOPING FLUENCY**   **PB** — **PROBLEM SOLVING**   **ES** — **EXAM-STYLE**

PS **1** Here are two circles. One circle has a radius of 5 cm.
The other circle has a diameter of 5 cm.

   a Find the ratio of the diameters.

   b Work out the ratio of their areas.

○○○

PS **2** A block of flats is in the shape of a cuboid. Nathan makes a scale
model of the block of flats. He uses a scale of 1 cm to represent 50 cm.

   a The height of the block of flats is 30 m. What is the height of
   the model?

   b The area of the front of the model is 300 cm². What is the area of
   the front of the block of flats?

   c The model has dimensions 10 cm by 25 cm by 30 cm.
   Find the volume of the block of flats.

○○○

PB
ES **3** Mario has a small photograph that he is going to enlarge on his
computer. The length of the small photograph and the length of
the enlargement are in the ratio 2:5.

   a Find the perimeter
   of the enlargement.

   b Find the area of the
   enlargement.

4 cm

← 6 cm →

○○○

138

DF **4** This cuboid has a surface area of 484 cm².

    a Find the height of the cuboid.

    b Find the volume of the cuboid.

    The cuboid is enlarged by scale factor 5.

    c Find the surface area of this cuboid.

    d Find the volume of this cuboid.

PB **ES** **5** The large watering can is an enlargement of the small watering can. The large can is twice the height of the small can. It takes Susan 30 seconds to fill the small watering can.

    How long will it take to fill the large watering can using the same tap?

PB **ES** **6** Lesley is designing a banner to advertise a concert. He designs this banner on his computer. The full size banner will fit across the doorway of the venue. The doorway has a width of 3.75 m. The banner costs £26 per square metre to make.

    Work out the cost of the banner.

Concert here Today — 3 cm, 7.5 cm

PB **ES** **7** Keith is making a model of a football stadium using a scale of 1 : 1000. The area of the base of the stadium in Keith's model is 2500 cm².

    a Find the area of the base of the actual stadium.

    The volume of the actual stadium is 10 000 000 m³.

    b Find the volume of Keith's model.

139

Geometry and Measures
Strand 6 3D shapes
Unit 7 Constructing plans and elevations

PS — **PRACTISING SKILLS**   **DF** — **DEVELOPING FLUENCY**   **PB** — **PROBLEM SOLVING**   **ES** — **EXAM-STYLE**

PS **1** Sketch the plan, front elevation and side elevation of these shapes. ●●○

a 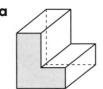   b 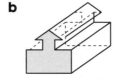   c 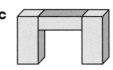   d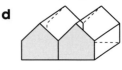

PS **2** The diagram shows the plan and elevations of a plinth. ●●○
Make an isometric drawing of this shape.

Plan 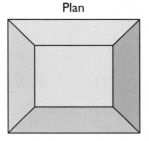   Front elevation    Side elevation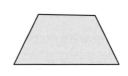

DF **3** The diagram shows a building. ●●○
ES Draw the plan, front elevation and side elevation.

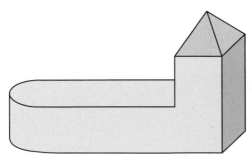

PB
ES
4 The diagram shows Emma's workshop.
The apex of the roof is central to the base.
The maximum height of the workshop is 3.5 m.
Draw an appropriate elevation to scale
and use it to work out the area of the roof
of the workshop.

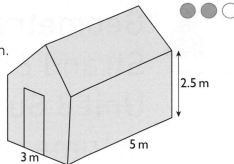

2.5 m

5 m

3 m

DF
5 The diagram shows an isometric scale drawing of a 3D shape.
The isometric grid is made with 1 cm triangles. 1 cm represents 5 cm.

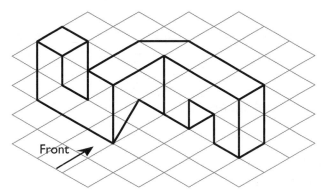

Front

Make an accurate drawing of the plan, front elevation and side
elevation of the shape.

PB
6 Here are the plan and elevations of a structure made from
toy building bricks.
The structure is made from:

- two cuboids with a square cross-section of side 4 cm and height 2 cm
- one cuboid with a square cross-section of side 2 cm and length 4 cm
- a square-based pyramid with a vertical height of 2 cm.

Draw the 3D shape on isometric paper.

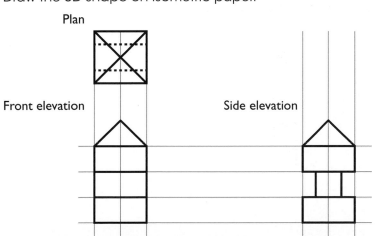

Plan

Front elevation   Side elevation

Geometry and Measures
Strand 6 3D shapes
Unit 8 Surface area and volume of 3D shapes

PS — **PRACTISING SKILLS**   **DF** — **DEVELOPING FLUENCY**   **PB** — **PROBLEM SOLVING**   **ES** — **EXAM-STYLE**

PS **1** Calculate the volume and surface area of a sphere with

    a radius 4 cm

    b diameter 7 cm.

    Give your answers correct to 3 significant figures.

PS **2** Work out the volume and curved surface area of a cone with

    a radius 5 cm, vertical height 12 cm, slant height 13 cm

    b diameter 12 cm, vertical height 8 cm, slant height 10 cm.

    Give your answers correct to 3 significant figures.

DF **ES** **3** A sphere has volume $36\pi\,\text{cm}^3$.

    Calculate the radius of the sphere.

DF **ES** **4** A cone with a slant height of 10 cm has surface area $40\pi\,\text{cm}^2$.

    Work out the radius of the base.

DF **5** This diagram shows a cylinder with a hemisphere stuck on top.
The dimensions are as shown.
Calculate the volume and the surface area of the shape.
Give your answer in terms of π.

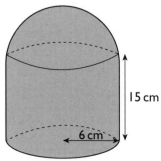

15 cm

6 cm

6 The diagram shows a shape made from a square-based pyramid placed on top of a cube of side 7.5 cm.

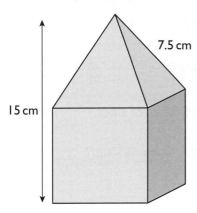

7.5 cm

15 cm

DF

a Work out the volume of the shape. ●●○

PE

b Work out the surface area of the shape. ●●●

7 The diagram shows a cube of side 10 cm with a circular hole of diameter 5 cm drilled through the centre.

Work out

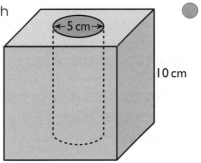

←5 cm→

10 cm

DF

a the volume

PE

b the surface area.

Give your answers correct to 3 significant figures.

8 The diagram shows the frustum of a cone. ●●○

It is made by cutting off the top of a large cone.

The dimensions are as shown.

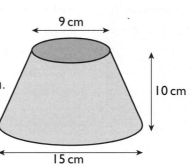

9 cm

10 cm

15 cm

PE

a Show that the height of the large cone from which the frustum is made is 25 cm.

DF

b Work out the volume of the frustum.

PE

c Work out the curved surface area of the frustum.

Give your answers correct to 3 significant figures.

PB
ES

9 A sphere of radius r cm has the same volume as a cone with a base radius of $2r$ cm.

   a Prove that the height of the cone h is equal to r.

   b What is the ratio of the surface area of the sphere to the curved surface area of the cone?

PB
ES

10 A company makes steel ball bearings by melting blocks of steel.
   The ball bearings are spheres with radius 0.25 cm.
   How many ball bearings can be made from a 1 m³ block of steel?
   Give your answer to the nearest thousand.

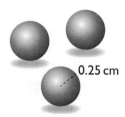

0.25 cm

PB
ES

11 Mr Field wants to buy a new silo to store the cereal crops from his farm.
   He has a choice of two cylinders. Both have a cylindrical base of diameter 20 m and height 20 m. Silo A has a hemispherical roof and Silo B has a conical roof.
   He wants to buy the silo with the greatest volume.
   Which silo will Mr Field buy?
   Show your working.

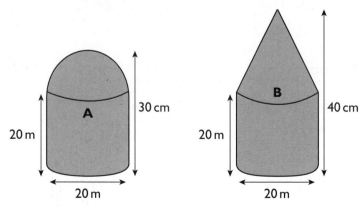

Geometry and Measures
Strand 6 3D shapes
Unit 9 Area and volume in similar shapes

PS – PRACTISING SKILLS   DF – DEVELOPING FLUENCY   PB – PROBLEM SOLVING   ES – EXAM-STYLE

PS 1 Two spheres have diameters in the ratio 3:5.   ●●○

    a Work out the ratio of their surface areas.

    b Work out the ratio of their volumes.

PS 2 The grey cylinder has been enlarged by a linear scale factor   ●●●
of 1.5 from the white cylinder.

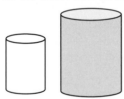

    a Write down the ratio of their radii.

    b Work out the ratio of their surface areas.

    c Work out the ratio of their volumes.

PS 3 Here are two similar children's building bricks. The grey brick is a   ●●●
linear enlargement of the white brick by scale factor 2. The volume
of the white brick is 20 cm³.

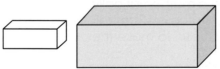

Work out the volume of the grey brick.

145

DF
ES **4** Here are two similar bottles of water. The small bottle holds one litre of water. The ratio of the heights of the bottles is 2:3.

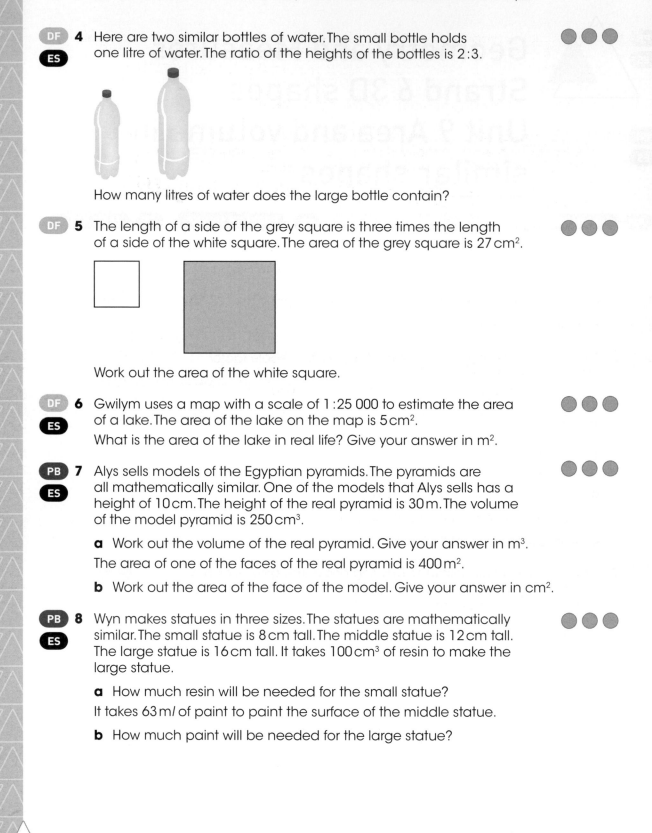

How many litres of water does the large bottle contain?

DF **5** The length of a side of the grey square is three times the length of a side of the white square. The area of the grey square is 27 cm².

Work out the area of the white square.

DF
ES **6** Gwilym uses a map with a scale of 1:25 000 to estimate the area of a lake. The area of the lake on the map is 5 cm².
What is the area of the lake in real life? Give your answer in m².

PB
ES **7** Alys sells models of the Egyptian pyramids. The pyramids are all mathematically similar. One of the models that Alys sells has a height of 10 cm. The height of the real pyramid is 30 m. The volume of the model pyramid is 250 cm³.

   a Work out the volume of the real pyramid. Give your answer in m³.
   The area of one of the faces of the real pyramid is 400 m².

   b Work out the area of the face of the model. Give your answer in cm².

PB
ES **8** Wyn makes statues in three sizes. The statues are mathematically similar. The small statue is 8 cm tall. The middle statue is 12 cm tall. The large statue is 16 cm tall. It takes 100 cm³ of resin to make the large statue.

   a How much resin will be needed for the small statue?
   It takes 63 ml of paint to paint the surface of the middle statue.

   b How much paint will be needed for the large statue?

PB **9** Phillipe makes models of the Eiffel Tower that are mathematically
ES similar. The small model has a height of 10 cm. The large model has
a height of 15 cm. It takes 120 g of metal to make the small model. Phillipe
has 360 g of metal.

Does he have enough metal to make a large model?

PB **10** Ffion is making solid podiums of two sizes for an awards ceremony.
ES The two podiums will be mathematically similar. The height of the small
podium will be 9 cm. The height of the large podium will be 15 cm.

The podiums are going to be made from concrete. The materials to make
the concrete for the large podium cost £62.50

a How much will the materials cost to make the small podium?

Ffion calculated it would take one tin of paint to paint the small podium.

b How many tins will she need to paint both podiums?

PB **11** A company makes plastic bottles. They make small bottles and
ES large bottles.

The small bottles have a height of 10 cm. The large bottles have a height
of 25 cm. The bottles are mathematically similar. The company has enough
plastic to make a million small bottles.

How many large bottles could the company make?

Statistics and Probability
Strand 1 Statistical measures
Unit 4 Using grouped frequency tables

PS — PRACTISING SKILLS   **DF** — DEVELOPING FLUENCY   **PB** — PROBLEM SOLVING   **ES** — EXAM-STYLE

PS **ES** **1** The table shows information about the weights of 50 onions.

Weight (grams), w	Frequency, f	Midpoint, m	$f \times m$
$70 < w \leqslant 90$	12	80	960
$90 < w \leqslant 110$	23		
$110 < w \leqslant 130$	10		
$130 < w \leqslant 150$	5		

   a In which group does the median lie?

   b Copy and complete the table.

   c Find an estimate for the mean weight.

PS **ES** **2** The number of complaints received by a TV company on each of 25 days is summarised in the table.

Number of complaints	Frequency, f	Midpoint, m	$f \times m$
0–2	3	1	3
3–5	11		
6–8	7		
9–11	4		

   a Copy and complete the table.

   b Find an estimate for the mean number of complaints.

   c Find an estimate for the range.

DF **3** In an experiment, some children were asked to do a jigsaw puzzle. The table shows information about the times taken to do the jigsaw puzzle.

Time (minutes), t	Frequency, f	Midpoint, m	$f \times m$
$5 < t \leq 7$	6		
$7 < t \leq 9$	18		
$9 < t \leq 11$	13		
$11 < t \leq 13$	8		
$13 < t \leq 15$	5		

a Write down the modal group.

b How many children did the jigsaw puzzle?

c In which group does the median lie?

d Copy and complete the table.

e Find an estimate for the mean time.

DF **4** In a land survey the areas of 90 fields are measured. The results are summarised in the table.

Area (hectares), a	Frequency, f
$0 < a \leq 10$	9
$10 < a \leq 20$	15
$20 < a \leq 30$	23
$30 < a \leq 40$	28
$40 < a \leq 50$	15

a Work out the number of fields with an area

   i greater than 30 hectares

   ii 40 hectares or less.

b Write down the modal group.

c Estimate the mean area of the fields.

PB **5** There are 100 trees in Ashdown Woods. The table gives information about the
ES heights of 85 of these trees.

Height (metres), h	Frequency, f
$0 < h \leqslant 4$	30
$4 < h \leqslant 8$	24
$8 < h \leqslant 12$	15
$12 < h \leqslant 16$	12
$16 < h \leqslant 20$	4

Here are the heights, in metres, of the other 15 trees.

3.5	10.3	11.4	6.7	3.9
4.2	12.5	2.4	15.8	17.0
9.5	8.9	14.9	15.2	7.8

a Draw and complete a frequency table for all 100 trees.

b Write down the modal group.

c Find an estimate for the mean height of the 100 trees.

PB **6** The manager of a shoe shop recorded the amounts of money
ES spent on shoes in one day. Her results are summarised in the table.

Amount spent (£), a	Frequency, f
$0 < a \leqslant 25$	4
$25 < a \leqslant 50$	26
$50 < a \leqslant 75$	63
$75 < a \leqslant 100$	17

a Work out an estimate for the total amount of money spent on
shoes that day.

b Find an estimate for the mean.

c Explain why this is only an estimate of the mean.

PB **7** Mrs Abdul takes some children to a theme park. The tables
ES give information about the heights of the children.

Boys		Girls	
Height (cm), h	Frequency, f	Height (cm), h	Frequency, f
$120 < h \leqslant 125$	0	$120 < h \leqslant 125$	1
$125 < h \leqslant 130$	3	$125 < h \leqslant 130$	3
$130 < h \leqslant 135$	7	$130 < h \leqslant 135$	8
$135 < h \leqslant 140$	16	$135 < h \leqslant 140$	15
$140 < h \leqslant 145$	9	$140 < h \leqslant 145$	8

a Compare the mean heights of the boys and girls.

One of the rides at the theme park has a height restriction.
Children with a height of 130 cm or less cannot go on the ride.

b What percentage of the children cannot go on the ride?

PB **8** The incomplete table below shows some information about the body
ES temperatures of the patients in a hospital.

Temperature (°C), T	Frequency, f	Midpoint, m	$f \times T$
$36.25 < T \leqslant 36.75$	15	36.5	
$36.75 < T \leqslant 37.25$	19		703
$37.25 < T \leqslant 37.75$		37.5	450
	10	38	380
$38.25 < T \leqslant 38.75$	4		

a Copy and complete the table.

b Find an estimate for the mean body temperature of the patients.

c In which group does the median lie?

A patient has a fever if they have a body temperature greater
than 38 °C.

d Find the best estimate for the number of patients with a fever.

PB **9** Balpreet recorded the lifetimes in hours, h, of some batteries. Here are her results.
ES

11.0	10.5	14.2	16.3	18.3	14.8	15.8	12.5	17.9	13.9
15.5	16.3	15.4	17.7	12.3	19.5	13.6	16.8	14.3	14.9
14.5	12.8	13.6	17.6	15.0	14.2	19.6	15.7	13.1	15.7

a Work out the mean lifetime of the batteries.

b Draw and complete a grouped frequency table for this data
using the intervals $10 < h \leqslant 12$, $12 < h \leqslant 14$, etc.

c Use your grouped frequency table to calculate an estimate for
the mean lifetime of the batteries.

d Is your estimate an overestimate or an underestimate of the mean
lifetime of the batteries? Explain why.

Statistics and Probability
Strand 1 Statistical measures
Unit 5 Interquartile range

PS – **PRACTISING SKILLS**　　**DF** – **DEVELOPING FLUENCY**　　**PB** – **PROBLEM SOLVING**　　**ES** – **EXAM-STYLE**

PS **1** For each of these data sets, find

　i the median　　　　　　　　**ii** the interquartile range.

　a −8, −5, −3, −2, −2, 0, 3, 5, 7, 8, 10

　b 3.6, 2.7, 4.8, 1.6, 8.3, 7.9, 6.8, 5.4, 3.3, 5.7, 7.0

PS **2** The box plot gives information about the lengths, in mm, of some worms.

　Find

　a the median length

　b the interquartile range of the lengths.

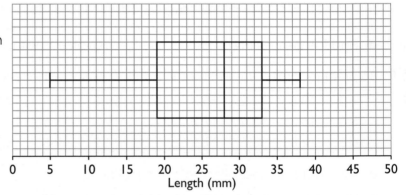

DF **3** The table gives information about the time taken, in minutes, to serve each of 80 customers at a supermarket check-out.

Time taken (t minutes)	$0 < t \leqslant 2$	$2 < t \leqslant 4$	$4 < t \leqslant 6$	$6 < t \leqslant 8$	$8 < t \leqslant 10$	$10 < t \leqslant 12$
Frequency	7	8	15	23	20	7

　a Draw a cumulative frequency diagram for this information.

　b Find an estimate for
　　i the median time
　　ii the interquartile range.

The shortest time taken to serve a customer was 0.5 minutes.
The longest time taken to serve a customer was 11 minutes.

　c Draw a box plot for the distribution of the times taken to serve these customers.

DF **4** The incomplete box plot gives some information about the weights, in kg, of some dogs. The diagram shows the lower quartile, upper quartile and highest weight. The median weight is 8 kg more than the lower quartile.

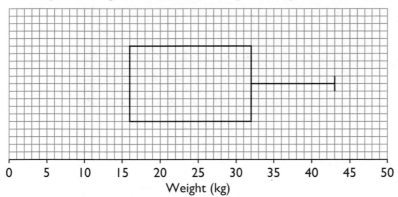

Weight (kg)

a Work out the median weight.

The lowest weight is 25 kg less than the upper quartile. Work out

b the lowest weight

c the range of the weights

d the interquartile range.

PB
ES **5** The box plots show information about the average number of miles per gallon (mpg) achieved by a sample of cars in 1990 and in 2010.

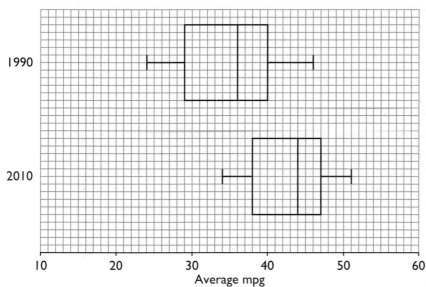

Average mpg

a Write down

i the highest average mpg in 1990

ii the lowest average mpg in 2010.

b Compare the medians and the interquartile ranges of the average mpg of these cars.

153

6 The cumulative frequency diagram gives information about the times taken by some children to do a test. More girls took 50 minutes to do the test than boys.

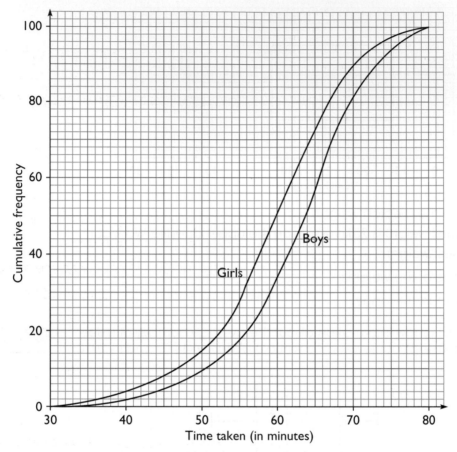

a Estimate how many more.

b Work out the percentage of boys who took more than 70 minutes to do the test.

c Compare the medians and the interquartile ranges of the times taken by these boys and girls to do the test.

Statistics and Probability
Strand 2 Statistical diagrams
Unit 4 Displaying grouped data

PS PRACTISING SKILLS   **DF** DEVELOPING FLUENCY   **PB** PROBLEM SOLVING   **ES** EXAM-STYLE

PS **1** State whether each type of data is discrete or continuous. The first one has been done for you.

    a The number of wheels on a bus
       discrete

    b The time taken to run 100 metres

    c The mass of an elephant

    d The number of bricks in a wall

    e The temperature of a cup of tea

    f The height of a mountain

    g The number of craters on the moon

PS **2** Copy and complete each category so that it has five equal classes.

    a $0 < w \leqslant 10$ $10 < w \leqslant 20$ ____   ____   ____

    b $100 \leqslant t < 150$ ____ $200 \leqslant t < 250$ ____   ____

    c ____ $15 \leqslant p < 17.5$ ____ $20 \leqslant p < 22.5$ ____

    d $125.7 < d \leqslant 126.2$ $126.2 < d \leqslant 126.7$ ____   ____   ____

    e ____ $2.5 \leqslant c < 2.8$ $2.8 \leqslant c < 3.1$ ____   ____

    f ____   ____ $0.56 < h \leqslant 0.6$ ____ $0.64 < h \leqslant 0.68$

PS **3** Neil has recorded the mass of 30 mice. Here are his results, in grams.

    12.7 20.7   15.3   22.8   21.3   18.4   15.9   22.1   19.9   13.5
    15.1 19.9   24.7   18.9   14.7   22.0   23.4   18.9   22.4   20.4
    20.4 17.2   19.5   17.3   19.1   19.7   17.9   21.8   14.1   16.4

    a Copy and complete the tally chart.

    b Write down the modal class.

Mass, m grams	Tally	Frequency
$12.5 < m \leqslant 15$		
$15 < m \leqslant 17.5$		
$17.5 < m \leqslant 20$		
$20 < m \leqslant 22.5$		
$22.5 < m \leqslant 25$		

DF **4** A doctor recorded the body temperatures of a sample of babies. Some of her results are in this frequency diagram.

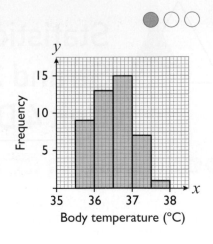

a Copy and complete the table.

b How many babies were in the sample?

c Work out the percentage of babies in the sample with a body temperature in the range $36 < x \leqslant 37$.

Body temperature, x °C	Frequency
$35 < x \leqslant 35.5$	0
	9
$36 < x \leqslant 36.5$	
$36.5 < x \leqslant 37$	
$37.5 < x \leqslant 38$	1

DF **5** Monica recorded the time taken, in seconds, to serve individual customers in her shop. Her results are summarised in the frequency table.

Time, t seconds	Frequency
$0 < t \leqslant 10$	4
$10 < t \leqslant 20$	8
$20 < t \leqslant 30$	17
$30 < t \leqslant 40$	12
$40 < t \leqslant 50$	9

a It took more than 40 seconds to serve some customers. How many?

b It took 17.5 s to serve Mr Brown. Which group is he in?

c Draw a frequency diagram to show the data.

DF **6** The stem-and-leaf diagram gives information about the heights, in metres, of 25 sycamore trees in a wood.

a Draw a frequency diagram to show the data.

b Describe the distribution. What, if anything, does this tell you about the ages of these sycamore trees?

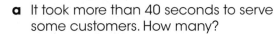

```
0 | 3  5  5  6  6  7  8  9  9  9
1 | 0  2  2  5  4  6  8  9
2 | 2  6  6  7  9
3 | 5  7
```

Key: 3|5 means a tree of height 35 m

PB **ES** **7** Amod recorded the lung capacities of 30 adult males. Here are his results, in litres.

5.6	5.7	5.1	5.9	5.5	5.6	5.1	5.6	6.8	5.3
6.1	5.4	6.2	6.4	5.4	5.7	6.4	6.5	5.9	6.4
5.8	5.9	6.3	5.1	5.8	6.6	5.6	5.3	5.8	6.8

   a Make a grouped frequency table for this data, using four equal class intervals.

   b Which class contains the median?

   c Draw a frequency diagram to show the data.

PB **ES** **8** Ori recorded the lengths of time, in seconds, some students could stand on their left leg. His results are in this frequency table.

Time (for left leg) t seconds	Frequency
$50 < t \leqslant 100$	12
$100 < t \leqslant 150$	33
$150 < t \leqslant 200$	20
$200 < t \leqslant 250$	8
$250 < t \leqslant 300$	7

He also recorded the lengths of time, in seconds, that these students could stand on their right leg. The results are in this frequency diagram.

Compare the lengths of time that these students could stand on each leg.

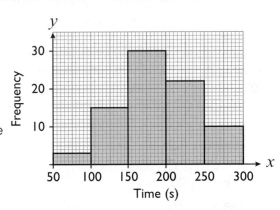

PB **ES** **9** Dafydd recorded the masses, m kg, of 300 babies. His results are in this pie chart.

   a Use the information in Dafydd's pie chart to draw a frequency diagram.

   b Cathy says, 'a frequency diagram is a better way to show Dafydd's results'. Do you agree with Cathy? Explain why.

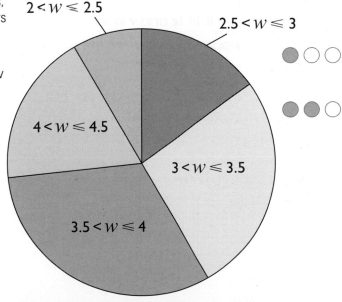

Statistics and Probability
Strand 2 Statistical diagrams
Unit 7 Histograms

PS PRACTISING SKILLS **DF** DEVELOPING FLUENCY **PB** PROBLEM SOLVING **ES** EXAM-STYLE

PS **1** Here is a list of types of diagrams.

bar chart **vertical line chart** **frequency diagram** **histogram**

Write down the diagram, or diagrams, from the list you would use to represent

a categorical data

b discrete data

c continuous data (equal class widths)

d continuous data (unequal class widths).

PS **2** Zach recorded the weights, in grams, of some mice. His results are summarised in the grouped frequency table.

Weight (w grams)	Frequency	Class width	Frequency density (frequency ÷ class width)
$5 < w \leqslant 10$	8	5	1.4
$10 < w \leqslant 15$	10	5	**i**
$15 < w \leqslant 20$	23	**ii**	**iii**
$20 < w \leqslant 25$	**v**	**iv**	3.4

a Find entries **i**, **ii**, **iii**, **iv** and **v** in the table.

b Draw a histogram to represent the data.

PS **3** Rhodri recorded the times, in minutes, it took him to travel to work.
The histogram shows information about his results.

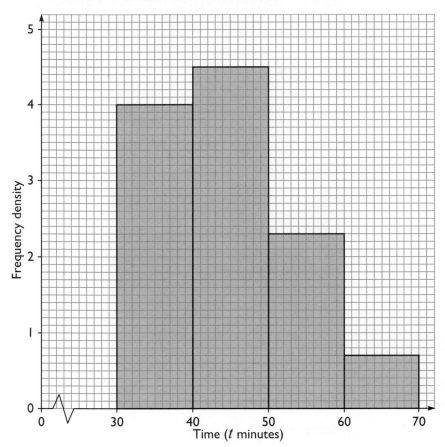

Use the information in the histogram to find **a, b, c, d, e** and **f** the table.

Time (*t* minutes)	Frequency density	Class width	Frequency (frequency density × class width)
30 < t ⩽ 40	4	10	40
40 < t ⩽ 50	**a**	10	**b**
50 < t ⩽ 60	2.3	**c**	**d**
60 < t ⩽ 70	**e**	**f**	**g**

PS **4** The histogram shows information about the speed of the water flowing in a river on each of 90 days.

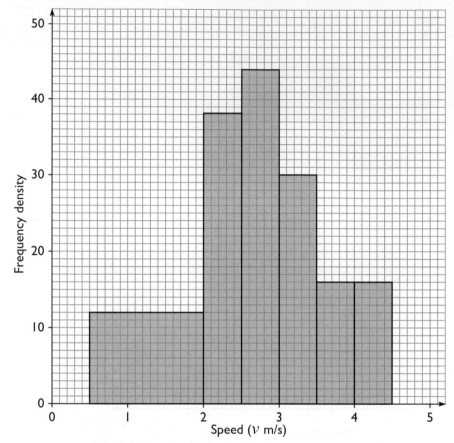

Draw a grouped frequency table for the information in the histogram.

Speed (v m/s)	Frequency density	Class width	Frequency (frequency density × class width)
$0.5 < v \leqslant 2$	12	1.5	18
$2 < v \leqslant 2.5$			
$2.5 < v \leqslant 3$			
$3 < v \leqslant 3.5$			
$3.5 < v \leqslant 4.5$			

DF **5** Fflur recorded the room temperature at 8 a.m. in her office on each of 90 days. The table gives information about her results.

Room temperature ($x°C$)	Frequency	Class width	Frequency density (frequency ÷ class width)
$10 < x \leqslant 15$	36	5	7.2
$15 < x \leqslant 19$	34	**i**	**ii**
$19 < x \leqslant 20$	8	**iii**	**iv**
$20 < x \leqslant 22$	12	**v**	**vi**

a Find entries for **i**, **ii**, **iii**, **iv**, **v** and **vi** in the table.

b Draw a histogram to represent the data.

DF **6** The cumulative frequency diagram shows information about the magnitudes of some stars.

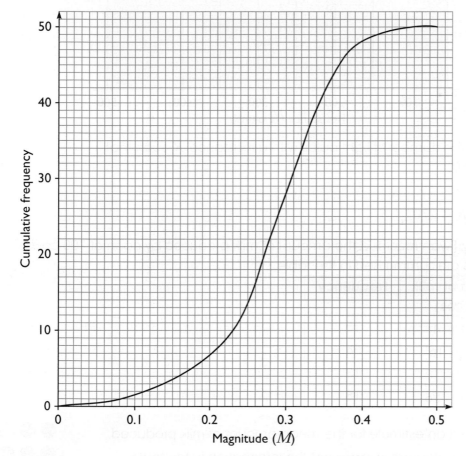

a Find

i the median magnitude

ii the interquartile range.

b Draw a histogram for the information in the cumulative frequency diagram. Use five intervals of equal width.

DF **7** The histogram gives information about resistances of some light bulbs.

ES

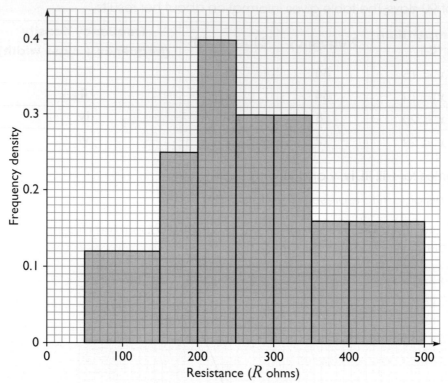

Work out the number of light bulbs with a resistance, R, such that

a $R \leq 150$

b $R > 300$

c $160 < R \leq 270$

PB **8** On Friday, Ewan recorded the amount of milk produced by each of 100 cows.

ES His results are summarised in the table.

Amount of milk (*a* litres)	Frequency
$0 < a \leq 4$	15
$4 < a \leq 16$	54
$16 < a \leq 18$	13
$18 < a \leq 26$	18

a Work out an estimate for the mean amount of milk produced.

b Draw a histogram to represent the information in the table.

PB **9** The histogram gives information about the heights, h cm, of a

ES sample of footballers.

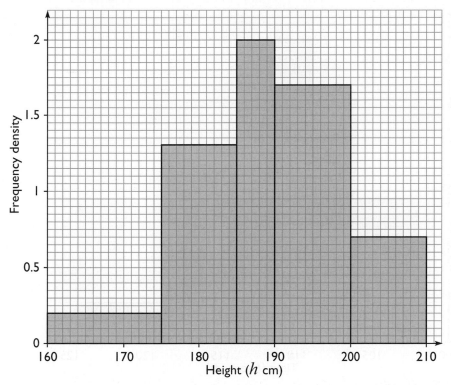

a Work out the total number of footballers in the sample.

b Work out the median height of the footballers.

One of these footballers is selected at random.

c Work out the probability that this footballer has a height greater than 190 cm.

10 Ipeto recorded the times it took some children to run up a hill.
The histogram gives some information about these times.

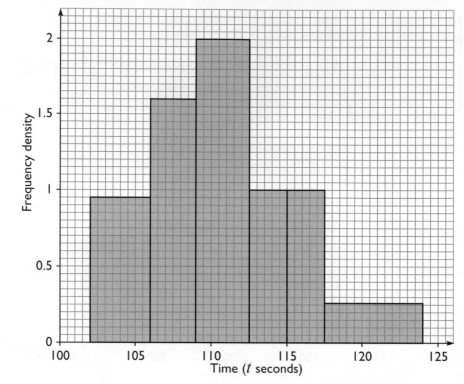

a Work out an estimate for the percentage of these children who took 110 seconds or more to run up the hill.

20% of the children took a time less than T seconds to run up the hill.

b Work out an estimate for T.

Statistics and Probability Strand 3 Collecting data Unit 3 Working with stratified sampling techniques and defining a random sample

	PRACTISING SKILLS		DEVELOPING FLUENCY		PROBLEM SOLVING		EXAM-STYLE
PS		DF		PB		ES	

PS
DF
1 Gareth wants to select a random sample of students from his mathematics class. He has the class list.

Explain why selecting every 3rd student will not produce a random sample of students from his mathematics class.

PS
DF
2 The number of members belonging to each of five rugby clubs is given in the following table.

Rugby Club	Number of members
Afongoch	250
Bryntor	580
Caebach	840
Hightown	150
Jonesville	100

25 members from across the five rugby clubs are to be selected. Use a stratified sampling method to calculate how many members there should be from each club. You must show all of your working.

PS
DF
3 A magazine editor wants to find out what proportion of the magazine's readers travel by train to work. She carries out a survey of the first 20 people carrying the magazine at 8 a.m. at the railway station.

Explain why this is not a good method of sampling.

PS
ES
4 The manager of a factory wants to investigate opinions of workers about sandwiches sold in the canteen.

On one day she asks the first 10 workers buying sandwiches their opinion.

a Explain why this is not a satisfactory method of selecting a sample of workers to ask about the sandwiches sold.

b Explain how the manager could select a random sample of 10 workers.

PS **5** A company employs people from a number of regions.

ES The number of people employed by the company in each region is given in the following table.

Region	Number of employees
North West	2345
North East	1657
South West	1282
South East	393

The company is organising a conference and decides to invite a total of 110 employees to represent the views of the all the people employed.

Use a stratified sampling method to calculate how many people from each region should be invited to the conference. You must show all of your working.

PS **6** An international sports charity has volunteers in Wales, Scotland, USA and South Africa.

ES The number of volunteers in each country is given in the following table.

Country	Number of volunteers
Wales	231
Scotland	92
USA	2352
South Africa	1123

The sports charity organisation is arranging an event and decides to invite 22 volunteers to represent the volunteers in Wales, Scotland, USA and South Africa.

a Use a stratified sampling method to calculate how many volunteers from each country should be invited to the event.

b Explain why South Africa would be sending only 6 volunteers, not 7 volunteers, to the event. Give two reasons for this decision.

Statistics and Probability
Strand 4 Probability Unit 5
The multiplication rule

PS — PRACTISING SKILLS   **DF** — DEVELOPING FLUENCY   **PB** — PROBLEM SOLVING   **ES** — EXAM-STYLE

PS 1 A box contains three blue pens and six black pens.

   a Celine takes a pen at random from the box. Write down the probability that the pen will be

   i   blue

   ii black.

   She puts the first pen back and takes a blue pen from the box.

   b How many

   i   blue pens

   ii black pens

   are now in the box?

   c Celine does not replace the blue pen and takes another pen from the box at random. Write down the probability that the pen is

   i   blue

   ii black.

PS 2 Bag A contains 3 red counters and 2 blue counters.

Bag B contains 2 red counters and 5 blue counters.

   a Copy and complete this tree diagram.

Catrin takes 1 counter from bag A and 1 counter from bag B without looking.

   b Work out the probability that both counters will be

   i   red

   ii blue.

   c Work out the probability that the counter from bag A will be blue and the counter from bag B will be red.

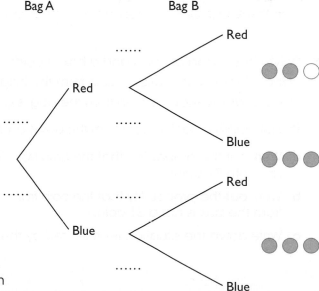

PS **3** Wyn has a fair five-sided spinner like the one in the diagram.
He is going to spin the spinner twice.

Work out the probability the spinner lands on

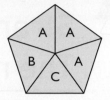

a A followed by A

b A followed by B

c B followed by C.

Wyn now spins the spinner three times. Work out
the probability the spinner lands on

d A followed by A followed by C.

PS **4** A box contains 7 lemon sweets and 6 lime sweets.

Mair takes 2 sweets from the box at random.
Copy and complete the tree diagram.

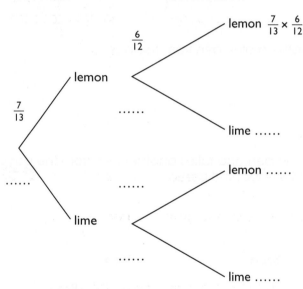

First sweet   Second sweet

lemon $\frac{7}{13} \times \frac{6}{12}$

$\frac{6}{12}$

lemon

$\frac{7}{13}$

......

lime ......

lemon ......

....

lime

......

lime ......

DF **5** Delyth has a bag of coins and a box of coins.

Without looking, she takes a coin from the bag and a coin from the box.

The probability that the coin from the bag is a £1 coin is $\frac{4}{7}$.

The probability that the coin from the box is a £1 coin is $\frac{3}{4}$.

a Work out the probability that the coin from the bag and the coin from the box
are both £1 coins.

b Work out the probability that the coin from the bag is a £1 coin and the coin
from the box is not a £1 coin.

c Write down the situation represented by the calculation $\frac{3}{7} \times \frac{1}{4} = \frac{3}{28}$.

DF **6** Tom and Simone both think of a number from 1 to 9 inclusive.

    a Work out the probability that they both think of

        i 3

        ii an even number

        iii a number greater or equal to 7

        iv a prime number.

    b Work out the probability that

        i Tom thinks of a number greater than 3 and Simone thinks of a number less than 5

        ii Tom thinks of a square number and Simone thinks of a prime number.

DF **7** Zoe takes two tests, A and B.

The probability that she passes test A is 35% and the probability that she passes test B is 85%.

The events are independent.

Work out the probability that Zoe will

    a pass both the tests

    b fail both tests

    c pass only one of the tests.

PB **ES** **8** Dilys and Mica are playing a game. They each need to roll a six on a normal six-sided die to start the game.

    a What is the probability that Vicky will start the game on her

        i first roll

        ii second roll.

    b What is the probability that Mica will start the game on his fifth roll of the dice?

PB **ES** **9** Sri wears a shirt and a tie to work.

The probability that Sri wears a white shirt is 0.8.

When Sri wears a white shirt, the probability that he wears a pink tie is 0.75.

When Sri does not wear a white shirt, the probability that he wears a pink tie is 0.35.

    a Draw a tree diagram to represent this situation. Fill in all the probabilities.

    b Work out the probability that Sri does not wear a pink tie when he goes to work tomorrow.

DF **8** Make a copy of the Venn diagram to answer each part of this question.

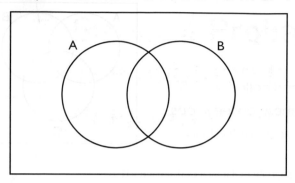

Shade the following regions.

a $A \cap B'$

b $(A \cup B)'$

DF **9** A food scientist is investigating different brands of muesli.

The two main ingredients she is interested in are pumpkins seeds and sesame seeds.
The food scientist analyses 50 different brands of muesli.
She finds 20 of the brands contain neither pumpkin seeds nor sesame seeds.
18 of the brands have pumpkin seeds and 22 of the brands have sesame seeds.

a Show this information on a Venn diagram.

b Estimate the probability that a brand of muesli selected at random will contain both pumpkin seeds and sesame seeds.

c Why is your answer in **b** only an estimate?

PB **10** Make a copy of the Venn diagram to answer each part of this question.

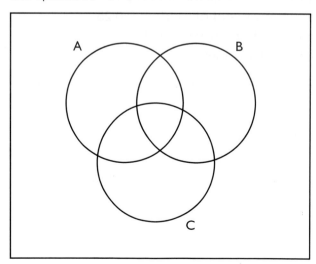

Shade the following regions.

a $(A \cap B) \cup C$ **b** $(A \cup B) \cap C'$

Statistics and Probability
Strand 4 Probability Unit 7
Conditional probability

PS — **PRACTISING SKILLS**   **DF** — **DEVELOPING FLUENCY**   **PB** — **PROBLEM SOLVING**   **ES** — **EXAM-STYLE**

PS **1** Tony has
3 red cards numbered 1, 2, 3
4 green cards numbered 1, 2, 3, 4
5 yellow cards numbered 1, 2, 3, 4, 5
Tony takes, at random, a red card, a green card and a yellow card.
How many different possible combinations of cards are there?

PS **2** A bag contains three red beads and five blue beads. Emma is
going to take at random two beads from the bag.

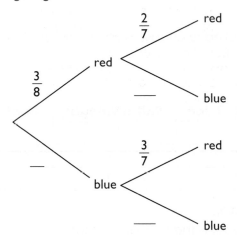

a Copy and complete the probability tree diagram for this information.

b Work out the probability that
  i both beads will be red
  ii both beads will be blue
  iii the first bead will be red and the second bead will be blue.

PS **3** In a survey, 25 students are asked if they are studying Geography and History. The Venn diagram gives information about the results.

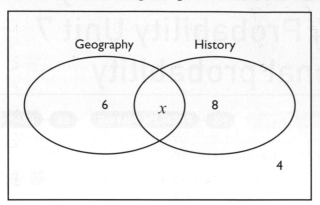

a Work out the value of x.

One of these 25 students is chosen at random.

b Given that this student is studying History, what is the probability that they are also studying Geography?

c Given that this student is studying Geography, what is the probability that they are also studying History?

DF **4** 79 people went on a trip. Each person was asked to choose a flavour of crisps for their lunch box. They could choose from Smoky Bacon crisps, Cheese & Onion crisps and Salt & Vinegar crisps. The two-way table shows information about the choices.

	Smoky Bacon	Cheese & Onion	Salt & Vinegar	Total
Male	15	11	13	39
Female	14	17	9	40
Total	29	28	22	79

Kim selects at random one of these 79 people.

a Given that the person selected is male, what is the probability that he chose Smoky Bacon?

b Given that the person selected chose Salt & Vinegar, what is the probability that they are male?

c Given that the person selected is female, what is the probability that she chose Cheese & Onion or Smoky Bacon?

d Given that the person selected did **not** chose Smoky Bacon, what is the probability that they are female?

DF **5** A box contains only black counters and white counters. A bag contains only black counters and white counters. Jim is going to take at random a counter from the box and a counter from the bag.

The probability that the counter from the box will be white is 0.4. The probability that the counter from the bag will be white is 0.7.

   a Draw a tree diagram to show all the possible outcomes.

   b What is the probability that both counters will be white?

   c What is the probability that both counters will be the same colour?

   d Given that both counters are the same colour, what is the probability that the counter from the box is white?

   e Given that the counters are **not** the same colour, what is the probability that the counter from the bag is black?

DF **6** Danni asked each of 50 people which, if any, of the three qualifying games of a football competition they had watched. Here is some information about her results.

22 had watched Game 1
29 had watched Game 2
14 had watched Game 3
5 had watched Game 1 and Game 3
7 had watched Game 2 and Game 3
12 had watched Game 1 and Game 2
3 had watched all three games

   a Draw a Venn diagram to show this information.

   b Danni is going to pick at random one of these 50 people. What is the probability that this person had watched Game 1 or Game 2?

   c Clive picked at random one of these 50 people. Given that this person had watched Game 3, work out the probability they had also watched Game 1.

   d Billy picked at random one of these 50 people. Given that this person had not watched Game 1, work out the probability they had watched Game 2 and Game 3.

PB
ES **7** A box contains three red pencils, four blue pencils and five green pencils. Steffan is going to take at random two pencils from the box.

Work out the probability that both pencils will be the same colour.

PB
ES **8** There are 11 girls and 8 boys in a chess club. Jake is going to pick at random a team from the chess club. The team will have two players.

Work out the probability that Jake will **not** pick two boys for the team.

PB **9**
ES

Tony has three bags of chocolates, bag A, bag B and bag C.

Bag A contains 3 dark chocolates and 5 white chocolates.
Bag B contains 2 dark chocolates and 7 white chocolates.
Bag C contains 4 dark chocolates and 3 white chocolates.
Sally is going to take at random a chocolate from bag A. If the chocolate is a dark chocolate she will take at random a chocolate from bag B, otherwise she will take at random a chocolate from bag C.
Work out the probability that she will take a dark chocolate and a white chocolate (in any order) from the bags.

PB **10**
ES

Here are some cards. Each card has a letter on it. Shelly is going to take at random three of these cards.

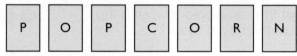

Work out the probability that two of the three cards will have the same letter on them.